Praise for Empty Cauldrons

"Empty Cauldrons stands alone in how. [illegible] through the poignant to the profound. Terence P. Ward has provided a unique work that while modern and cutting edge also flows like a timeless grimoire, exploring ancient magic and formula that is not only invaluable to whom may be challenged by depression but those immersed in the healing arts and community for a better understanding of those we support, work with and love. Empty Cauldrons supersedes anything of the like I have ever read, a truly unique and altering read."

—Witchdoctor Utu, founder of the Dragon Ritual Drummers
and author of Conjuring Harriet "Mama Moses" Tubman
and the Spirits of the Underground Railroad

"Few works in our communities have set about tackling this topic, for as Ward states plainly, depression is an antagonist that does not like to be talked about ... [Ward does] an admirable and soulfully necessary job of breaching the boundaries of the looming elephant in our room—depression—as a serious medical condition, wrought with obstacles not just within the throes of its tendril'd unfolding, but from without in a society which systemically shifts from vantage upon them, and these. From topics of suicide to stigmas inside and out, this book compassionately (and with temperance) implores readers to sit with their biases and fears, examining the realities of an oft under-examined element of harrowing impact in the lives of so many today."

—Theanos Thrax, author/scholar,
mental health consultant, polytheist priest

"I don't say this lightly or often—this is an important book, not only for the community that is its target market but for anyone who is living with depression. Empty Cauldrons is a rare gift to anyone who has been looking for answers to the shadowy questions that haunt them—it's readable, sensible, hopeful and effective. Get it. Gift it. Give thanks for it."

—H. Byron Ballard, priestess and pastor,
author of *Roots, Branches and Spirits*

"A remarkable undertaking addressing what it is to have chronic depression and to be pagan... Ward, a well-known pagan journalist, has assembled his personal journey into a deep yet accessible discussion of how depression affects our spirituality and how our practice may help us address depression. He brings perspectives from many pagan leads who he interviewed for this work. While reading this I found myself thinking, I should order a couple dozen copies for people I've known and counseled over the years and their families."

—Rev. Dr. C. Davis Sprague, MD, HP Stewart Tradition

"Depression isolates us from all that we love. With *Empty Cauldrons*, Terence Ward helps break that isolation through courageous truth telling and a thoughtful, practical approach to a range of Pagan spiritual tools. Ward brings together a multiplicity of voices and traditions, creating something more than a mere self-help book with a Pagan twist. Encompassing storytelling, devotionals, spellcraft, and above all, a deep respect for the wisdom traditions of Paganism, he has created a book that belongs on the shelves of any Pagan who has struggled with depression, or who knows someone who has. I cannot recommend this book strongly enough."

—Cat Chapin-Bishop, MSW, LICSW,
author of *Quaker Pagan Reflections* and
founding chair of the Pastoral Counseling
Department at Cherry Hill Seminary

empty
cauldrons

About the Author

Terence P. Ward is a journalist and practicing Pagan for more than thirty years. He has been bound to a Wiccan coven, communed with the earth as a backpacking Pagan (aka Gaiaped), and been tapped by the Olympian gods. He manages his depression through his work as a priest to Poseidon in Temenos Oikidios, a Rhode Island-based Hellenic temple. Ward is also a member of the order of the occult hand, and is a minister ordained through the Church of the Sacred Earth: a Union of Pagan Congregations in Vermont.

Navigating
Depression Through
Magic and Ritual

empty
cauldrons

Terence P Ward

Foreword by M. Macha NightMare

Llewellyn Publications
Woodbury, Minnesota

FIRST EDITION
First Printing, 2022

Cover design by Shira Atakpu
Editing by Marjorie Otto
Interior art by the Llewellyn Art Department

Llewellyn Publications is a registered trademark of Llewellyn Worldwide Ltd.

Library of Congress Cataloging-in-Publication Data (Pending)
ISBN: 978-0-7387-6333-0

Llewellyn Worldwide Ltd. does not participate in, endorse, or have any authority or responsibility concerning private business transactions between our authors and the public.

All mail addressed to the author is forwarded but the publisher cannot, unless specifically instructed by the author, give out an address or phone number.

Any internet references contained in this work are current at publication time, but the publisher cannot guarantee that a specific location will continue to be maintained. Please refer to the publisher's website for links to authors' websites and other sources.

Llewellyn Publications
A Division of Llewellyn Worldwide Ltd.
2143 Wooddale Drive
Woodbury, MN 55125-2989
www.llewellyn.com

Printed in the United States of America

To Pan Ganesha,
whose life's journey was not ended by depression,
although it was surely shortened by its presence.

Contents

Contents

Exercises

Strategies for Spirit

Rituals and Routine

Prayers, Offerings, Dreams, and Spells

Acknowledgments

It's a little bit daunting to think about all of the people who make it possible to write a book, because like every other part of the human experience, it's only possible in community. I am humbled and grateful to be one of this amazing species, despite all mistakes we make trying to live and and learn about this wondrous world. Nevertheless, there are certain individuals whose presence and influence helped wrest these ideas from my brain and put them to page for others to share.

Robin Ward, my unflappable life partner, whose faith in my capabilities and potential have never wavered.

Heather Greene, my editor, who has the gift to recognize the really good stuff in the first draft that I wrote and help to bring out its shine.

The many people who took the time to talk to about their own expertise and experience: Anthony Rella, Barbara Rachel, Courtney Weber, Ivo Dominguez, Jr., Joshua Tenpenny, Kelden Mercury, Kirk White, Nimue Brown, Orion Foxwood, Raven Kaldera, Sarah W., and Siobhan Johnson all gave generously of their time and attention with no reward promised. Without them, this book would have been flat and without life.

Perhaps most important, I give thanks to the many people whose stories are not included, either because they were unwilling to share such personal information, or because they later got cold feet and withdrew consent to use the material. Your struggles are the reasons this book needed to be written.

Disclaimer

Neither the author nor any of the interview subjects, except where noted, are licensed to practice medicine, offer counseling, or prescribe medication in any jurisdiction. What's presented here is personal opinions based on the experience of individuals, and if the reader finds wisdom in these words then that is a blessing. However, no material herein is a substitute for medical advice from a licensed professional, because no medical doctor or therapist can provide the personal advice you may need without knowing about your history and circumstances.

Please, please, *please* consult a professional if you are struggling. If you feel that you are in immediate danger to yourself, call the National Suicide Prevention Hotline at 800/273-8255. More resources are in the back of this book.

Foreword

One of the big "secrets" that Paganism shares with society at large is the bugaboo of depression, or as I prefer to call it by the ancient Greek word *acedia*. Whether you call the condition depression or acedia, this state is difficult to describe. Acedia is a spiritual staleness, emptiness, ennui.

It's a common affliction yet it carries an undeserved stigma, so it often remains invisible to others. Symptoms of the mind and spirit tend to be viewed as evidence of weakness or moral failing. That has certainly been the case in my family and in the society in which I was reared, and I'm sure it's a common attitude. As a result, an individual suffering from depression doesn't usually reveal that fact.

In recent years, society at large has recognized the reality of depression as a fairly common affliction. Depression is becoming more visible and less taboo. It's always been there, but now it's being addressed.

Depression affects us emotionally, physically, and spiritually—body and soul. We become sluggish and our thinking becomes cloudy. We forgo physical movement and exercise. We often eat poorly, with no attention to proper nourishment. We may sleep and sleep and sleep, and still be fatigued. This neglect results in our becoming weaker in every way. We shun the company of others and we retreat into solitude.

Weakness and isolation create a vicious cycle that feeds itself and continues unabated. However, it can be managed and overcome. With social contact, outside help of whatever kind(s), and supreme effort, this spirit of ennui can be starved.

Western medical professionals utilize the prosaic method of treating the body with various medications intended to restore sufferers to a less anxious and more grounded state. This is combined with talk therapy, both individually with a psychiatrist, psychologist, or social worker, as well as in groups. In my experience, the latter reaps the greater reward. Others may find it difficult to remain open, honest, and trusting in a group setting and prefer individual therapy.

This is fine and good, but limiting treatment to these methods alone neglects the spiritual dimension.

Pagans respect and appreciate science and the scientific method, yet we want and need to include treatment of the spiritual dimension in the healing process. We, and I, hold as a truth that all sufferers of depression require a more holistic approach, one that brings together our different parts. Only by engaging the whole person, all these dimensions, in the healing process can we restore ourselves to wholeness and health.

Although I address my remarks to an assumed pagan or paganish readership, the methods suggested in this book can be useful to anybody of any religion or no religion at all.

Terence Ward experiences episodes of depression, as do I. In this book he offers us the benefits of his own struggles with this specter of a black dog. And he hasn't done it alone. Knowing that our communities hold an abundance of creativity and wisdom, he questioned other pagans who have suffered this affliction. Some of his interviewees walk the same path as he, while others travel parallel or diverging paths. He wanted to learn about their own episodes of *acedia*. He asked them what approaches to healing they might have used in dealing with their depression that they found efficacious, and incorporated their insights into this book so that we can have the benefits of what they found valuable in their efforts to recover and heal.

The more techniques for healing from depression that we have, the better. What works well for one individual may not be helpful to someone else. One or several methods may appeal to you, while others may not.

We mustn't overlook the value of community and social connections. You can work with others to heal depression. Or you can take some comfort by participating in ritual for other unrelated purposes, such as celebrating a sabbat. Take some time to get out of yourself and into relationships with others.

Among various approaches to healing, and in addition to physical exercise and a health-promoting diet, the author suggests exercises such as keeping a mood journal to help us name our problems.

Generally speaking, we pagans have a self-help, DIY mindset rather than a passive acceptance of conventional remedies. We espouse self-reliance. We value agency and empowerment, although we don't feel either when we become sunken with depression.

As a long-time traveler on a pagan path, I learned that the way to address issues is to speak of them, to lay them on the table, and then to figure out what engenders the problem. An occurrence such as a death, a situation, a seemingly impossible task, a long-term or life-threatening illness. In other words, to name them. By naming them we can have some control over them. We can address them directly.

We can apply the same method to depression when we see it as a spirit—naming it and gaining control/agency.

We can do the same by honoring the spirit of any medication, by speaking to it of our intention, and by asking for its aid.

We pagans often have already established relationships with one or more personal deities from whom we can seek aid. We may also look to divine personages associated with healing. Some examples are the Greek Asclepius, whose serpent-draped staff is still a symbol of medicine today, and/or his daughters Hygeia and Panacea, from whose names we get the English words hygiene and panacea "cure-all." Deities of healing springs and wells can help, such as the Yoruba Orisha Aja, or Sulis whose healing waters are at Bath.

Christians who seek healing can appeal to the Blessed Virgin Mary, Mother of God.

My personal preference, a goddess with whom I've cultivated a personal relationship and who has many wells and shrines in Ireland, is Brigit. I have a candle honoring her on the shelf above my desk as I write this.

Further, I am a person who gets satisfaction from the act of performing ritual. As the late priestess of Hekate, Tara Webster, has said:

"Ritual works with metaphoric and archetypal symbols that circumvent the verbal defenses our minds put up to protect us from the pain of the issues we cling to.

Ritual work can bypass the defenses that keep us from being able to heal! The same defenses that protect our pain also keep us from being able to access it, release it, and heal it."[1]

She affirms the efficacy of remedies proposed in this book:

"As a psychotherapist I've worked with people for years and have watched them try various anti-depressant medications and not make

---

1. V. Vale and John Sulak, *Modern Pagans: Investigation of Contemporary Practices* (RE/Search Publications: San Francisco, 2001), 109.

much progress. But I've seen people cured of life-long depression using ritual. I believe you can get value from both practices."[2]

Depression is disorienting in itself so it needs to reinforcement. Therefore, whatever methods you employ should all have a gentle approach.

There is a supremely apt word that the author coined that I've adopted. The term is "revivicide." Revivicide means recommitting to life. Let us all revivicide.

Terence has brought the topic out of the broom closet and into the light of day. And he's done it in a magical way that can offer understanding and foster healing. I am grateful to him for this gift and I'm sure you will be, too.

M. Macha NightMare (Aline O'Brien)
Lughnasad
San Rafael, California

---

2. V. Vale and John Sulak, *Modern Pagans: Investigation of Contemporary Practices* (RE/Search Publications: San Francisco, 2001), 109.

Introduction

I didn't want to write this book. If you experience depression, you probably wouldn't want to either. There is a certain quality of depression that makes it hard to name, hard to discuss, hard to acknowledge. It is easier to look away from depression, whether it's impacting a coworker, a family member, or oneself. I didn't want to write this book because depression doesn't like to draw attention. That's part of why I see depression as having agency and refer to it as a spirit—albeit using an admittedly broad sense of that word. I have not determined whether depression is something external that moves in, or some sort of personal egregore, or a part of the soul that has drifted away, or even a part of the soul that is doing exactly what it's supposed to be doing. However, it's not about the intent; it's about the impact.[3] Whatever its reason for existing, depression brings harm.

Despite the inclination never to discuss it, I have always wanted to discuss it. In 2014 I wrote a post in my blog about depression being a spirit, publishing it just before the winter solstice. I shared

---

3. Melanie Tannenbaum, "'But I Didn't Mean It!' Why It's So Hard to Prioritize Impacts Over Intents," *Scientific American*, October 14, 2013, https://blogs .scientificamerican.com/psysociety/e2809cbut-i-didne28099t-mean-ite2809d- why-ite28099s-so-hard-to-prioritize-impacts-over-intents/.

my "warm fuzzies" story about depression (a version of which is in this book) as a way to express my frustration with how people always seem to miss the mark when gauging the seriousness of depression in others. It's a condition that can be dismissed as something to be "shaken off," but it can also trigger hyper-vigilance in loved ones who fear death by suicide. The result is actually the same: it feels like people are looking at you differently. It would not be fair to blame someone else—even someone else who has had experiences of depression—for getting it wrong, because depression is something people don't wish to talk about, and when we do not speak of an idea then words atrophy around it. Just take a look at definitions for depression: they are always long, and sometimes contradictory. It's hard to pin down and it's easy to misunderstand. People who are very familiar with depression might not even know what it is, and scientists can write for pages trying to explain it.

For me, and likely for others, there is an ebb and flow to depression. (I am a devotee of Poseidon. I use a lot of ocean metaphors.) How that ebb-flow cycle manifests for me has changed over the years, because my relationship with depression has evolved. At times, I've felt it getting stronger as the nights grow longer, beginning with a tickle of doubt crawling up my spine around the time of Lughnasadh. Sometimes, the pressure of obligations I have made—to humans, to gods, even to my pets—builds up before me and makes forward movement increasingly difficult, like a ship pushing too much water. External events can always trigger a depressive event, but how well grounded I am in myself can inform how traumatic that event will turn out to be. I give myself the time to slow down and focus on myself, because if I do not the outcome won't be a good one. I am affecting the condition as much as it affects me. Depression is never in control even when it may feel like I am not; it can feel like moving the planchette across a talking board with a friend: are we both in control, is it neither of us, or is something else entirely?

Every person has biases, and I name anyone who claims the ability to set them aside a fool. My preference is to name the biases I know I carry, to make it easier to tease them out of the words I use and the interpretations I offer. I invite my readers to do the same, particularly when experiencing a strong reaction to anything in this book. Curiosity can be helpful in this; ask why the words elicit a particular reaction, and patiently follow that thread to understand what in one's own experience helped inform it. I have no desire to be hurtful with any words I choose, and I pray never to bring harm in my ignorance.

I grew up in the 1970s and 1980s in what one of my teachers termed a "lily-white community." I am a male human with a relatively pale complexion, and most of my ancestors going back twenty generations hailed from northern Europe. (Perhaps a quarter of them were from Asia Minor and nearby, but I grew up accepted as a white person in the United States in the latter part of the twentieth century.) I have never struggled with my gender identity, although my gender was misidentified once by a person who was so gobsmacked by the error that it became the sole focus of the remainder of a very awkward conversation. I have only been physically assaulted once by someone because of my perceived identity, because I can pass in many white communities, and I avoid others. I am a homeowner with pets but no genetic children, and I have been a recipient of government aid more than once in my life. I am a priest of Poseidon and a member of the Society of Friends, colloquially known as Quakers. I practice conjure, I meditate, and I spend more time than is healthy scrolling through social media and watching television. I walk with privilege that is sometimes invisible to me, and I walk with depression, which is often invisible to everyone.

Pagans are about as hard to pin down as depression, and that's challenging for an author seeking an audience. If I am to be authentic, I may only write what I know. Rather than inviting the reader to choose a divine source that suits their own inclination, I will always insert my own. I trust that anyone who follows a clear tradition should have no problem adapting the core intent of my ideas to conform with those practices or, if that proves impossible, to ignore that material entirely. That is because the conscious mind will zero in on what's different, and automatically start chewing on how to change those parts out. If you have no clear idea what path you follow, I can relate because I walked the poly-traditional path myself for a very long time. I hope that you find something that resonates with you in these words, dear reader.

This is a book about looking at a pervasive condition through the eyes of magicians, spirit workers, polytheists, animists, and witches. pagans spend a lot of time discussing their differences from one another, but there are values that I believe are common enough in our overlapping subcultures that we could even say that we share them. One of those is the belief that science does not contradict our religions, because myths are understood not to be literal. Depression can—and should—be understood in terms of medical science about the brain and the mind. Those of us who are open to religion and mystery do not need to dismiss science, any more than a trained scientist is required to reject religion simply because it cannot be consistently validated through the five senses. Science and religion engage different parts of ourselves, and bringing together our different parts is an important part of healing. That's why *also* looking at depression in terms of its impact on the spirit, soul, and different aspects of the self is important. The mind has incredible potential for self-correction, and just because we do not always understand how these mechanisms work does not mean that they don't work.

While I am a journalist, this book is not purely journalism. I did interview several people who possess experience with or knowledge about depression, trying to collect viewpoints about its causes and its management from a wider perspective than just my own. These include Courtney Weber, Kirk White, Siobhan Johnson, Raven Kaldera, Sarah W., Nimue Johnson, Anthony Rella, Joshua Tenpenny, Kelden Mercury, Barbara Rachel, Ivo Dominguez, Jr., and Orion Foxwood; there are short biographies for them all in the back of this book. With their assistance, in the first part of this book— depression in the world—I have created a picture of depression that draws upon both science and religion in an attempt to describe the nature of our relationship with it. Exercises for a journal are included at the end of each chapter. The second part—strategies for life with depression—contains a heavy helping of exercises to explore, understand, and alter that relationship. This includes rituals and spells to try.

Keeping a Journal

Humans are different from all the other beings I know about, in part because humans can write things down. That is a powerful way to solidify an idea, and the face of the world has been changed by this ability. A way to harness this gift is by keeping a journal. Thoughts that feel out of control can be caught by the pen, and held fast on paper to study from a safe distance. Written thoughts are frozen at the moment of creation, the key to a memory of that idea. To write is magic, and for that reason some people make no distinction between a journal and a book of shadows. The regular use of either one should help you better understand and influence the world around you.

I recommend keeping a journal as a tool for understanding the experience of depression. The benefits are high, and the risks can be managed. Journals can be used in different ways, and the exercises in this book are examples of a few different styles. If you're just starting to use a journal and you're also in a period of depression, it might be easier to pick only one focus for your journal, because having too many options is not always a good thing. Here are a few approaches to consider. If you find a journal exercise later in the book that has a different focus than your own journal, you can feel free to skip it. There's also information about expanding how you use your journal later on in the introduction.

Ways to focus a journal:

- *Moods only:* It's perfectly acceptable just to jot down a word or two describing your mood, as described in the section on tracking moods.

- *Pain dump:* Awful memories can rise to the surface during depression, as Courtney Weber describes: "Sometimes my first thought [upon waking] is guilt and remorse over something I said in fourth grade," she explained. "'You're the worst person in the world,'" the voice of depression affirms. Those memories are pushed through a filter that strains out everything nice or positive, and then they swirl around as the mind ruminates, raising the dark cone of power that seems to sustain the spirit of depression. Get those thoughts out of your head by committing them to words. If possible, put them on paper and use the writing implement as a wand to direct the negativity out of you and freeze it in the words themselves.

- *Log of affirmation:* Take a moment to center and ground, and then commit to writing one positive affirmation in the same way you might word a spell: "I am delightful company." "Laundry is a task that comes easily to me." "I am intelligent and thoughtful." "My contributions are valuable to those in my community." If you're inspired to go on to expand on what that looks like, go right ahead—but remember to maintain that positive image throughout.

- *Naming symptoms:* Anthony Rella describes using a journal to identify and assess the severity of symptoms, as a way to objectively decide if it's time to get help. If you're unsure if you need to talk to a counselor or therapist, "commit to spending thirty days identifying a particular problem you're struggling with and tracking it in a journal or a spreadsheet … you could start by just writing down everything you find challenging, or habits that are causing you unhappiness, and try to distill them down into behaviors you can track. This part would be tricky, but if you are able to identify something like, 'I think about killing myself,' 'I only sleep three hours every night,' or, 'I don't leave the house because I'm worried about what people will think of me,' then those are relatively objective and observable. Then for thirty days, keep track of how often the behavior happens. At the end of the month, look at what you've got and see how you feel about it. If you have Xs for these behaviors that are causing you unhappiness more days than not and you don't want to keep living that way, find a therapist."

- *Storybook:* Myths and stories speak to our subconscious, the younger self, the id. Joshua Tenpenny found that when seeking the source of one's depression, "I'd always pick the least changeable circumstance as the cause of my misery." That's not surprising, because a mind laboring in depression is always going to gravitate to the worst possible thoughts.

That's how depression rolls. Why not choose to write a different story? Instead of trying to answer a loaded question such as "Why am I such a pathetic person?" look for a tale that tackles something simpler such as "Why do I have this weight on my chest?" Maybe an absentminded gremlin left an invisible weight on you while you slept, and if you ask nicely, the gremlin will remove it. If you're more pragmatic, that weight might be a reminder that you need to check the pressure in your tires. Once you finish writing that story, check the pressure in your tires to signal your subconscious that the weight may now be lifted. This is fiction, and you can tell any story you like. The best stories are ones that leave you feeling more in control—aim for a happy ending. That part of your being that responds to stories has been given permission to work on healing by bringing your condition in line with the story.

- *Dear depression:* Take the "dear diary" approach and write entries to the spirit of depression directly. "Today I lied to my best friend. I claimed I had a migraine and couldn't go out for drinks because I just wanted to lie down. You suggested I stay home with *Downton Abbey* and two pints of ice cream, and then you suggested I lie about it because it's just easier. Am I really that good company, depression? I am not so sure, and I was thinking that maybe we should see other people."

Writing tends to be easier to do the more one does it, but if you sit down with an open journal and a blank mind, try starting with one of these prompts:

- What color is today?
- If my emotions were an animal, what could I feed to it other than myself?
- Where do I hurt?
- Did someone hurt me today? How may I forgive them?
- What was my first thought upon waking, and how do I feel about it?
- What has made me angry today?
- If I were to write a thank-you note right now, who would I thank and what would I say?
- Which god do I want to be watching over me right now?
- If I have a long-forgotten ancestor who understands how I feel right now, what do I imagine about that's person's life?
- Make up an origin story for your depression. The condition was made possible by many factors that probably stretch out over years, but stories can be healing even if they are not factually complete. Create a short story describing the birth of your spirit of depression.
- What myths could be told about depression, its agenda, how it was created, or when it has spent time with others in the past? What role does it play in history? How does it choose its host? Is it a protector or a punisher by design? What does it look like outside of the body? Is depression a single spirit, or are there many spirits of depression?

There is nothing wrong with expanding the purpose of a journal, as long as it's done with intent. Otherwise, you might find yourself ducking out on your journal and then feeling guilty about it. Review your writing from time to time to make sure that your purpose has not drifted—a log of affirmation can easily become a pain dump without the writer noticing, or you might realize that you're demanding so much of yourself that the journal is becoming a source of pain, rather than a release from it. If you wish to avoid this "journal bloat" when you add to or change the purpose, then set a new intention and consider starting a new book. You could also divide it into sections for different types of entries.

❧ EXERCISE ☙
Releasing a Journal

If the practice of keeping a journal is feeling overwhelming, it's okay to lay that down as a way to control journal bloat. This exercise can be used on a general-purpose journal, or a separate book or section that has a specific intention.

What you'll need:

- The journal you wish to release.
- A length of string that is about twice as long as the measure of the journal (measuring the height, width, and thickness).
- If what you're releasing is a section of a larger book, then instead of using string you'll need a stapler with staples that can go through all the pages.

What you'll do:

1. Hold the book, or grasp the section, and say, "Thank you, journal, for being a place where I record my thoughts (about _____). At this time, I ask too much of myself and cannot use you at this time. I release you from all expectations of receiving new thoughts from me."

2. Seal the journal to formalize that you are not expected to update it. Tie it around both directions with the string or, if it's just a section of a larger book, staple the pages together on all three sides. Say, "I seal this journal against all eyes, save my own if and when I choose."

3. Store the sealed journal in a secure place until you wish to look at it, or burn it if you wish.

You can always start a new journal when you're ready, or unseal an old one to continue it. The purpose of this exercise is to free you from any sense of failure or guilt about a journal, making it easier to pick up the practice again later.

The section on strategies for the body and mind has information on different ways to protect a journal from prying eyes.

My hope for each person reading this book is to bring a recognition that depression is not condition over which one has no control, but a relationship that can be altered. I expect that this understanding will be as uncomfortable for some as it has been for me, because rediscovering your own agency requires overcoming deeply-seated beliefs. I cannot make that leap for you, but I will be waiting on the other side.

Terence P. Ward
New Paltz, New York

part one
Depression
in the World

one
Defining Depression

Depression is a condition that can be hard to pin down. Scientists have tried to define it with technical language and poets have taken a stab at it as well. Depression can be explained emotionally, spiritually, and biochemically; no matter what words are used to describe it, depression is something you know best by experiencing it.

Here's how major depressive disorder is explained in the *Diagnostic and Statistical Manual of Mental Disorders*. (The DSM, as it's called in shorthand, is a stupendously large book that lays out current thinking about how to describe all manner of mental conditions in medical terms.)

The individual must be experiencing five or more symptoms during the same two-week period and at least one of the symptoms should be either 1) depressed mood or 2) loss of interest or pleasure.

- Depressed mood most of the day, nearly every day.
- Markedly diminished interest or pleasure in all, or almost all, activities most of the day, nearly every day.
- Significant weight loss when not dieting or weight gain, or decrease or increase in appetite nearly every day.

- A slowing down of thought and a reduction of physical movement (observable by others, not merely subjective feelings of restlessness or being slowed down).
- Fatigue or loss of energy nearly every day.
- Feelings of worthlessness or excessive or inappropriate guilt nearly every day.
- Diminished ability to think or concentrate, or indecisiveness, nearly every day.
- Recurrent thoughts of death, recurrent suicidal ideation without a specific plan, or a suicide attempt or a specific plan for committing suicide.[4]

Not everyone finds this definition particularly helpful. It includes a lot of wiggle room that might lead to misdiagnosis of someone suffering from a different condition, for example. It's also exhausting to read through and understand if you're already experiencing a "slowing down of thought." The list of symptoms included therein "could have more than one cause, and the cause might not respond to the usual treatment recommendations," according to psychiatrist Bick Wanck.[5]

Common English isn't exactly helpful in describing depression, either, because depression is a slippery concept. "I think it's a poverty of the English language that we use the same word to describe how a five-year-old feels when his baseball game gets canceled because it's raining and the way someone feels who's about to jump off a bridge because life has become unlivable and untenable," said writer

4. Jessica Truschel, "Depression Definition and DSM-5 Diagnostic Criteria," Psy.com, accessed November 12, 2020, https://www.psycom.net/depression -definition-dsm-5-diagnostic-criteria/.

5. Bick Wanck, *Mind Easing* (Deerfield Beach, Florida: Health Communications, Inc., 2019), 31.

Andrew Solomon in a 2014 interview.[6] "It gets used to describe such a range of experience, it's sometimes difficult for people who are dealing with acute clinical depression to convey how different their circumstance is from the circumstance of someone who's simply sad." That makes depression slippery, because it's hard to confidently pin down what we mean by the word. Clinical and scientific definitions are precise in part because they are narrow; that's the way of words. Depression resists that level of rigor, and thus it takes pages and pages to explain what's even meant by the word.

Nevertheless, trying to narrow down that clinical diagnosis is not going to be productive because depression does manifest in a lot of different ways, and many of them are similar to what one might endure on a bad day. Social worker Barbara Rachel laid out when a person might need some help to deal with things, saying that symptoms are "depressed mood every day with marked decrease in enjoyment in activities that used to be enjoyable; change in eating with either weight loss or gain; insomnia or oversleeping every day; appearing slowed down or agitated to observers; a sense of tremendous fatigue; feelings of worthlessness or inappropriate guilt; difficulty concentrating or deciding things; and most seriously, recurring thoughts of death, plans to commit suicide or actual failed attempts." Rachel further explained that taken together, these symptoms might become hard for a person to handle alone. "All these symptoms cause serious impairment in functioning, such as at a job or taking care of the home or self. All of these symptoms may occur in reaction to a severe loss of some kind and would be considered a normal reaction, but if they are prolonged or are deeply troubling, this is a sign of a problem."

---

6. Solomon, "'Darkness Visible' Broke Ground."

Siobhan Johnson, a writer and witch practicing in England, "was presenting with low mood, brain fog, social isolation, lack of drive, poor hygiene, insomnia and irritability, suicidal ideation, bingeing, and withdrawal from life. It appeared to others as a range of things including worms, of all things." There is not, as of this writing, a way to satisfy the human desire to define depression's causes and symptoms in concrete terms. It's incredibly frustrating to have one's symptoms defy a diagnosis because a diagnosis gives hope for a treatment. I can't speak to what sort of working definition professionals were using when Johnson was first seeking treatment, but that account suggests that a condition that is hard to define can also be hard to diagnose.

One might be resistant to the idea of being in depression too. "Unless you are an experienced diviner and can actually ask, don't try to decide if what the client has is depression, or what sort of depression it is," warned shaman Raven Kaldera. "Just go with what they're saying. You can ask, 'Do you think you're feeling depressed? Any idea why?' Depression is a touchy subject and it's hard to get around one's opinions on the subject. If you are an experienced diviner, have something in your divination system that indicates clinical depression, perhaps in a particular context. I have mentally marked out an appropriate card in one of my tarot decks, and asked the gods and spirits to let that be an indicator of clinical (and likely chemical) depression, and to push me intuitively toward using that deck for the client if that's a message they need to hear. When it occasionally comes up for a client, I know this is a big flag and I'm supposed to pay attention."

What depression is *not* is ordinary sadness, something that can typically be shaken off, or your fault. Depression is quite often a life-long companion, with at least half of the people who live through one period of depression experiencing a second, and an even greater portion of those who are depressed twice experiencing it yet again. There are two pieces of good news in that last sentence: the first is that half of people who experience depression never will again, and the second is that depression does not kill most people anyway. Living a fulfilling life is possible even if depression comes to visit more than once, and the skills to manage it have been learned by many people.

Depression is "something I'll always deal with," says Courtney Weber, a witch practicing in the northwestern United States. "The negative thoughts in my head, the actions from that, such as picking on the dog, just comes out of nowhere. I get visions of things I did and it's proof I'm a bad person. No, it's not true; the disease is telling me something not true. I would not fault a child for doing bad things; I'd ask what's wrong in the kid's life," and to evaluate one's own life more harshly is to use a double standard.

Trauma can get passed from one generation to the next, too. Weber's great-grandmother ended up being a single mother full of "terror and sorrow," Weber has learned, and impressed upon Weber's grandmother the importance of not living life and rearing a family alone. "She put fear into her daughter: you must be married, do not take this journey alone. At that time, this meant meeting standards of beauty, and led to an obsession with thinness and a strange relationship with food that has been taught down the line." It's not about whether people in your family tree suffered from the condition so much as whether people in your family tree experienced the sort of trauma that might *contribute* to suffering from depression. Even if Weber's great-grandmother weathered her pain without experiencing depression, the lessons she learned and handed down had lasting effects for years to come. Add in other lessons from other ancestors and the convergence can produce conditions conducive for depression to be born.

"When I was around thirty, I came to terms that some things won't change," says Joshua Tenpenny, a pagan living in the northeastern United States. "I work around the things that don't work," such as developing the mental discipline to navigate through life when desire and motivation are absent. It isn't chronic for everyone who experiences it, but many people do have recurring symptoms, and in the most profound cases it can be disabling. It does not mean that there is no hope. It does not mean that life is devoid of happiness, or meaning. Even if it's chronic, depression can be managed and overcome. Being aware of tendencies to withdraw from the world and having a game plan that other people can help you enact if that comes to pass is important. It's dangerous to go it alone.

Does depression have a purpose? "I think it's a glitch," said Tenpenny. "Stuff in the modern world may make it worse. I don't think it has a meaning, but one can learn from any experience, including that of suffering. It gives compassion for others, and understanding, but that's pretty easy to learn. The idea of a greater purpose is not meaningful for me."

Searching for the cause of depression feels important for many people, but it's often a fruitless quest. Some of us feel like it's easy to control something if we can place it in context, but the search for a cause in some ways is a search for blame. During depression, any hunt for blame tends to lead to either a) I am a terrible person who deserves all the suffering I endure, or b) all others are terrible people who treat me unfairly, or perhaps a combination of the two. Runaway, ruminative thinking and negative self-talk has a way of turning this quest into an albatross. It's normal to have curiosity about what led to this experience, but telling someone that their lung cancer was caused by smoking a pack a day for forty years isn't going to cure the condition, is it?

Depression does not automatically mean that one is contemplating suicide or has an unhealthy relationship with one or more drugs, but those risks are very real, especially in people who do not have other tools for dealing with depression. Those of us who have had more than one bout of close contact with depression usually become better at identifying the signs: dwelling on negative memories, unexpected emotional outbursts, changes in our ability to think clearly or engage in even the simplest of tasks. There is evidence that older people are happier people,[7] which suggests to me that eventually I'll reach the point of putting a stop to it even before it begins again. Not the life anyone chooses to lead, but as author and psychotherapist Kirk White told me during one of my darkest periods, "The secret to life is living. The rest is just details."

Weber, Tenpenny, and I all have this as a chronic condition, and one of the common threads is that it often manifests in early adolescence. Situational depression can also bring one's life to a full stop, but for some people it can completely go away through some combination of time and treatment. Complicating matters still more is the fact that someone with chronic depression can also experience situational depression. There is much muddying of communication when it comes to these topics, and sometimes it makes people feel like they are experts when they are not. Perhaps depression's original home was the tower of Babel.

The ambiguity of language has led to a number of methods to try to be more precise when referring to depression. That might mean discussing more narrowly-defined conditions such as seasonal affective disorder and persistent depressive disorder (formerly called dysthmia), comparing chronic and situational depression,

---

7. Association for Psychological Science, "Why Are Older People Happier?" Last updated January 5, 2012, https://www.psychologicalscience.org/news/releases/better-research-is-needed-to-understand-why-elders-are-happier.html.

contrasting the chemical from the clinical depression, or separating passing emotions from an ongoing condition by using terms like "being depressed" and "in depression." Is it clear which of those last two phrases refers to someone who is very sad, and which points to an individual who is moving through a murky morass of emotional sludge for a period of years? No, it is not, and no matter how precisely I choose to define terms in this book there will be others who use them slightly differently, rendering my efforts moot. The use of terms varied even among those I interviewed for this book, and any attempt to shoehorn them into my arbitrary definitions would not improve clarity. The reason there is not an intuitive distinction between the concepts is because it does not serve depression to be easily described.

An estimated 264 million people experience depression, according to a 2018 study.[8] More than a quarter of a billion people yet it eludes a clear definition to help pin it down in common language. During my interviews, depression was compared to fog, water, a black cloud, darkness, silence, cold, and heaviness; those who have experienced it feel isolated, slowed, silenced, smothered, invisible, and exposed. Some have directly compared it to death—imagining that death must feel something like depression—or surmised that death could not be worse, or that living through depression and living through a journey to the underworld might be similarly difficult.

The therapist with whom I had the longest relationship described depression as "anger turned inward." It's simplistic, but that doesn't make it wrong.

---

8. Spencer L James, Degu Abate, Kalkidan Hassen Abate, Solomon M. Abay, Cristiana Abbafati, Nooshin Abbasi, Hedayat Abbastabar, et al. "Global, Regional, and National Incidence, Prevalence, and Years Lived with Disability for 354 Diseases and Injuries for 195 Countries and Territories, 1990–2017." The Lancet: 392:1789-1858. https://doi.org/10.1016/S0140-6736(18)32279-7.

"Depression for me is a sort of inner death, or numbing out, or being in a place where I just can't feel anything good any more," said British Druid Nimue Brown. "It can take any of these forms and can move about between them. It goes with a loss of energy, a lack of motivation and inspiration, an inability to hope or believe in anything good. It messes with my concentration as well. This is awkward for me because I'm invested in the idea of myself as a creative, capable sort of person, so there's a loss of self when this comes round."

"Depression feels to me like a numbness, like a great horrible weight that saps all of your energy," said Johnson. "You can't think straight, and you distract yourself almost out of instinct. It's easy for self-hating thoughts to run on a loop, but what really stands out in my experience of depression is that numbness, and the self-sabotaging behaviour isn't really a punishment when you get down to it; it's just something to make you feel again. Good feelings like joy and pride seem too hard, but tiredness from staying up too late, the buzz from food or video games or music or alcohol, physical pain, mental strife—that's easier to get hold of. You'll make up any kind of rules to give yourself an excuse for punishment, because it reminds you you're alive."

Author and conjure-man Orion Foxwood describes depression's symptoms as a "state of emotional deflation ... a leaky tire that can't ever be patched enough," with no motivation to do anything about it or most anything else. This tends to be coupled with a sense that "everyone wants us away from them," even as people try to help, which itself can trigger guilt and shame for being such a bother. It's an unkind cycle: those who wish to help often don't know how to, or presume all it will take is a little support for someone as they "pull themselves out of it," but people with depression may need much more. Foxwood has personally experienced serious depression, triggered by high levels of pain during a crippling bone malady that required a replacement of both hips to address, which itself left him with large debts.

Sarah W. likened depression to shaman sickness, a trauma that marks the spirit worker. The term "shaman"—which is often identified with spirit work generally—comes from indigenous Siberian tribes, and some feel using the term is cultural appropriation. Shaman sickness is a form of illness that takes the worker to the brink of death and perhaps allows for a crossing into the underworld; upon recovering, the spirit worker should possess knowledge of illness or death that can be used to heal others. Some mythological *katabases*—descents into the underworld—are evocative of depression directly or indirectly. Inanna must strip herself bare to visit the underworld, which may be easy to imagine for someone who has experienced depression. Demeter's grief and, arguably, depression when her daughter is in the land of the dead is attributed as the cause of winter. In seeing this as a chronic condition, "I come to view it as my version of a shaman sickness," Sarah W. explained. Sarah W. does not feel like it's been inflicted by a god or spirit "to teach me a lesson, but I can choose to see it as something I can learn from. ... It's a catalyst for a lot of development."

When my first teacher accepted me as a student, I said that I wanted to learn to be a shaman. I did not bring this sickness upon me by asking to learn to be a shaman—a term I no longer use for myself because it is infused with that specific context—rather, I was starting to become aware of a trial I was already enduring, and I was asking for help.

Depression can be described as draining color from life, but Tenpenny adds nuance to the metaphor by distinguishing between the black depression and the grey. "Mine is grey," he said. "Nothing is interesting, don't want to do anything." One might say that depression is associated with an imposed stillness, and the inertia of that stillness is profound.

Tenpenny can enjoy an activity if he engages in it, but "the desire, the wanting is gone. I have no wants; they're all dead." Even though he'll enjoy the activity, when depressed he finds motivation is a "big struggle," and the more difficult the task, the mightier that struggle. Even getting out of bed can be challenging.

That brings to mind another of the ways Sarah W. described the experience of depression, calling it by the ancient term *acedia*, "a spiritual staleness, emptiness, boredom, the 'noonday demon,'" which is "not quite the same as the clinical" understanding of depression. "It could be called fallow times, or the dark night of the soul."

On the other hand, Wiccan author Ivo Dominguez, Jr. contrasts the monochrome of depression with the vibrant colors of practicing magic. Dominguez likens depression to the crossed conditions that are a focus of hoodoo and root work, but also sees it as a curse. "Your own powers of manifestation, turned against yourself, bringing into being the worst outcomes," something of a spiritual hijacking. There are similarities between depression and crossed conditions, Dominguez explained, or "at least a strong overlap between the two. There is a spiritual component in that regard, to some degree there is externalizing of inward gloom." Similarly, White says that in the context of Chinese medicine, depression might be seen as an "inability to manifest."

"I look at depression as malady, ally, and aftershock," Foxwood said. Malady is the condition of depression itself, together with its panoply of symptoms. It can be an ally, he said, "if we can surf its tides, go deep without losing ourselves, swim in those waters without being lost; [when we] get clarity we become an oracle for the deep place, the underworld, for healing." Depression is also aftershock particularly for those who are sensitive to subtle beings and energies, because "gods and their people have been wounded horrifically," and some people "cannot ignore that and engage in even the components of Paganism. The ancestors still cry out for redemption."

Yet another way to conceive of depression was explained to me by Minnesota-based Norse cultural educator Kari Tauring: that depression exists because the parts of the soul become disconnected, one from another. In Norwegian, *hug* is a concept Tauring likens to "heart-mind-soul" in English, and *huglaus* refers to being depressed. "It's the mind, heart, and spirit loosened, not in alignment, that is what creates depression," she said. It's as if depression exists in the space between the soul-parts, perhaps because there should *be* no space there. It occurs more often in times of physical darkness, but also times of "blighted thought." The three components of *hug* "can't find each other," leading to "no spark" or ability to rekindle one. Moreover, "someone else's gumption is not what it takes" to set it alight again.

Tenpenny is not always in tune with emotional responses during periods of depression. That does not mean emotions are absent, as I once believed; rather, when emotions are expressed they can catch a person by surprise. While emotions can be triggered by thoughts, they come from the body and are closely connected to the instincts which are built into our genetic code. Try this experiment: grit your teeth, clench your fists, and breathe quickly and shallowly. You've created an emotional response, without involving the brain. A lack of awareness of emotions is a symptom of the disconnection that Tauring describes, and there's nothing quite like being caught off-guard by anger, or love, or fear, to make one feel disconnected from everyone around them too.

Anger was Weber's constant companion as a young adult, and as with Tenpenny, it wasn't always clear why. "I was always angry, but I didn't know the source," Weber said. This transitioned into abusive relationships. "Someone being nice was uncomfortable; there must be something wrong with them." Weber came to prefer romantic partners "who mocked my degree, or the fact that I hadn't read *The Sound and the Fury*," she said. She recalls one of these partners once observing, "You're not very pretty, but I like you anyway." As a Christmas present one year, she received a handwritten copy of Shakespeare's "My Mistress's Eyes Are Nothing Like the Sun," which is anything but complimentary. Weber's self-esteem was low enough to make it easy to accept such treatment as par for the course.

In Chinese medicine, the question asked is often "Where is the energy not flowing?" White associates depression with the element of wood in the Chinese system, which controls fire, the flow of chi. With depression, that flow is interrupted and builds pressure inwardly. This covers symptoms like brain fog and low motivation, while the related buildup of pressure speaks to symptoms such as self-harm and outbursts of anger.

The question Foxwood raises is "Why is it always bad to feel sad?" It can be reflective of times shared with a departed loved one, for example, an opportunity to give that person respect expressed through grief and mourning and memory. "Not all deep places are places where we drown," he said, but demonizing of the underworld can make it harder to accept that truth in the deepest parts of self. "We've lost reverence for deep emotions," he laments. "I'm not sure all pains should heal, and that all depressed states are to be avoided. In fact, most should be given time to be." He describes it as being "summoned by your soul. It wants us quiet and uncontaminated, and it has something it wants to say." Depression can be "the magnetic, cool call of the soul," while its frequent companion anxiety might in fact be "the electric hot call of the spirit" that "people don't know how to recognize. They are forms that are debilitating, but would not be if we weren't taught to resist the low places." That resistance causes harm that might be avoided by leaning into it, in his view. Anger has its place, and neither honoring that place nor expressing that feeling is ever good for one's health. "I want to re-sacralize rage," he said, "because volcanoes can build new land."

"I pretty much managed up until fourteen or fifteen, where the brain fog really presented itself," recalls Johnson. "I had glasses made to try to keep me focused in lessons; I do have dodgy eyes, but that wasn't the cause. My grades started a slow decline— I was top of the class to the point of boredom anyway, so it wasn't really caught until too late—and then I was told off for not studying. I got Cs and Bs, but not the As I was predicted. This is the period that my hygiene and social life pretty much vanished as well. The bullying got worse, and I was minorly molested almost every school day by a fellow student. Again, my memory is really foggy, but I do remember my mother not being able to make an appointment with anyone at school regarding it, so one day she and I literally just stood in the foyer until someone talked to us. Nothing came of it, and that whole episode was bungled several more times." For Johnson, depression resulted in behaviors that marked a difference, like poor hygiene and poor grades. This in turn led to bullying, similar to how some animals will drive off a member of their group when a perceived flaw is deemed dangerous to the whole.

For Brown, "All of this has roots in stuff that has happened to me, along with pain and exhaustion as reliable triggers. I tend to have a fair idea of what's going on, which means I can at least tell other people about that, and it takes the pressure off them a bit. Part of what causes this is low self-esteem—I'm easily knocked down and have a hard time picking myself up, and in part it's because I don't reliably feel that I deserve nice things, or happiness. I've spent significant chunks of my life persuaded that my basic human needs were just selfish wants, while the things I wanted were so off the scale as to make me a terrible human. Times when crying because I was hurt would be responded to like I'd just launched a massive attack on someone [and] this kind of thing leaves marks. If I'm feeling fragile, I still find it hard to tell if the things I imagine I need are things it might be acceptable to need. This means I am not always well equipped to look after myself. Knowing about it helps, but I'm still not reliably able to sort it out."

One reason depression can be more challenging to deal with in some western cultures is because of what Tauring calls "one of the most dangerous things our western culture has produced," the observation by philosopher Rene Descartes of "cogito ergo sum" ("I think, therefore I am"). "It was the moment when we pulled ourselves completely apart," Tauring believes, by concluding that the mind is "the sum total of who we are," leaving no room for other aspects of self. The Nordic concept includes thought and memory as parts of the soul, she explains, and both "are connected at the heart's root," which she contrasts with the modern western perspective that prioritizes treating symptoms of the body, and tends to frame symptoms of the mind and spirit as evidence of weakness or moral failing: "Those [who are] struggling [are] seen as weak and damaged, and not in control of their humanity."

Another modern shift in thinking Tauring thinks contributes to depression is how time is conceived. Norse "ancestors were past-looking, and believed we are creating the past as we go. Old Norse didn't even have a future tense, with the nouns not representing past, present, and future but rather is, is becoming, and lastly debt/necessity/should. "We think of the future in terms of debt to the past, or what precedence tells us is appropriate action." Much anxiety and depression might be alleviated by people getting unstuck from planning for the future without using the past as a guide for what might be.

My understanding of depression is drawn on my own experience, as well as the experiences of those who were kind enough to agree to be interviewed about it. The experience of pain, loss, and the pairing of sadness and grief can be useful in understanding depression, because those emotions can be as painful and intense. What separates grief from depression is the ending and the beginning. No matter the intensity of grief, it has an end. There will come a time when the death of even the closest loved one will not sear the soul with constant agony. The idea of an ending feels much less certain with depression, and I think that has more to do with the beginning. We know the origin of grief, but for depression it's less certain. Sometimes it's possible to identify a moment that feels like the beginning of depression, but there were always many other moments before it, moments that built up stress and taxed the emotional reserves. We all have different levels of resilience, and they change over time as do other factors that contribute to health and well-being. Once we reach and exceed whatever our personal stress threshold might be, depression might settle in.

It was when I lost a college friend to suicide that I learned how grief and depression can differ. We had been out of contact for many years, reunited thanks to the surging interest in social networks that happened in the latter half of the aughts. We liked, commented, and sent each other messages from time to time, but plans to reunite in person were never made. When I got news that my friend had committed suicide, I was gripped with a powerful sense of grief and loss. I blamed myself for not trying harder to connect, wondering if I could have said the one kind word needed to prevent this from happening. Having been through depression and having taken the path of suicide a good long way, I felt that perhaps I ought to be an expert, with the power to detect these troubles in others and to eliminate them. It turns out that the experience of depression has left me with no such gifts. Thoughts of our relationship consumed me for days, and my ability to perform household tasks or paid work was significantly curtailed as I mourned. Then, gradually, the paralyzing weight of sadness lifted as I processed those emotions.

Years later, I am still very sad about this loss of life, but those memories do not sting or crush any longer. I will never know what drove my old friend to that decision, and I can but hope that the suffering ended. My pain has healed in a way that my friend's did not, and I believe that this is because depression had a hard grip on my friend, and it was too much to bear. I know that grief can last much longer than it did in my story, but it is expected to soften, reduce, and in time fade away. Depression, often without beginning, feels unending. That thought itself can be a bit depressing, but rest assured there are millions of people in the world who have found ways to manage their periods of depression. That effort is sometimes frustrated by all of this ambiguous language.

We are storytellers, and depression defies that part of our nature too. It's not easy to tell a tale that has no beginning, and no end. Stories connect with different aspects of the self than analytical information. If only the conscious mind is engaged, the ability to resist is limited. We lack myths about depression, stories that speak to this shared experience and how they can be addressed. There are certainly myths in the other sense of the word, that of "an unfounded or false notion."[9] Here's a story that fits more into the latter definition:

---

9. Merriam-Webster, "Myth," accessed April 17, 2021, https://www.merriam-webster.com/dictionary/myth.

Back before the turn of the century, I attended a high-level healing ritual that gave me a surge of hope and a crash of disappointment. College had flamed out for me in the wake of being hospitalized in the middle of a semester. I didn't quickly recover from that low point, but eventually found myself living with my parents, working a semblance of a job, and returning to school part-time. As part of my studies, I was awarded a grant to go to a particular pagan conference and write a paper about it. I had a support system of family and friends, my education had resumed, and my life was turning in a positive direction.

At this conference were a goodly number of people whom I didn't know were important until many years later. The centerpiece seemed to be this particular healing ritual, held after all the other programming was wrapped up for the day, and included at least fifty people. The facilitator directed energy raised by the attendees to effect healing, and the impact was often quite dramatic. It was a multi-hour affair, and some had to take a break or be excused before it was all over.

Early on in the evening, a "triage" of needs was undertaken. In other words, this powerful healing was available to all. This was high-grade stuff, helping people with cancer and heart disease and profoundly debilitating conditions. I was only about two years past having been locked up for trying to kill myself, and even after I started getting treatment I had since been through a period of over a month when I would remain in bed for up to twenty hours a day. I, too, had a life-threatening, profoundly debilitating condition. That's what I shared.

I received a smile, and then, "We'll do that at the end, with the warm fuzzies."

That well-regarded elder had bought into the myth that clinical depression is the same as passing sadness. If someone has had a super-sucky day that started with bad coffee and an empty gas tank and never quite improved, warm fuzzies can probably scrape that gunk off the aura. If warm fuzzies are not enough for people enduring cancer and other life-threatening conditions, they are not going to cut it with depression. Confusing it with a passing phase—or a moral failing—will do nothing to solve the problem, and could well make it worse.

When it comes to depression, we do not lack for myths in the sense of common misconceptions. There are deeper myths, too—the ones that speak of the relationship with depression through allegory or metaphor. The condition is not new, and while I do not know of any tale describing a depression demon, for example, the many underworld journeys speak of a loss that might feel familiar: there are Greek (Orpheus and Persephone), Sumerian (Inanna), and Egyptian (Osiris) tales about experiencing loss—of possessions, or memories, or something else that is precious—when crossing into the land of the dead. A Greek myth tells of how Sisyphus sought to cheat death, and as a punishment was forced to perpetually push a boulder uphill, beginning anew when it rolled back down. I can think of no better description of the sense of exhaustion and futility that settles on people during depression. *Acedia* and *melancholia* were both terms used by the ancient Greeks to describe symptoms now considered depression: it was being observed and named. It may be time to revisit old myths to bring out their lessons about depression, or discover new ones tuned to that purpose.

Another quality that separates depression from strong negative emotions is that it does not always get processed like an emotion, which would allow for healing. Instead, a voice of destructive self-talk emerges in the psyche, a voice that is extremely critical. Weber eloquently described being reminded of reasons why one is not a good person who deserves happiness or healthy relationships, undermining things that weaken depression such as wholesome foods, movement of the body, and social connection. It might be described as a feedback loop, but I instead see it as a dark cone of power being raised from these negative emotions. Michael Pollan writes about research that suggests that some mental conditions "are not the result of a lack of order in the brain but rather stem from an *excess* of order. When the grooves of self-reflective thinking deepen and harden, the ego becomes overbearing. This is perhaps most clearly evident in depression, when the ego turns on itself and uncontrollable introspection gradually shades out reality."[10]

Johnson goes on to say that "it was explained to me more along the lines of fear and anxiety/depression as a means to keep yourself safe. If I want friendship, but I don't have it, clearly I'm rejecting it in some way. The isolation and withdrawing because of depression is actually a safety mechanism that's overdoing it, to try to keep me from being rejected/hurt/abused. I think that actually a lot of mental illness is kind of an autoimmune disease of the mind—it's the mind overreacting to an initial trauma, however big or small, and then finding more and more triggers to react to."

The authors of *The New Mind-Body Science of Depression* posit that depression is indeed connected to immune response. Whether that's proven scientifically or not, it's a useful model for thinking about depression, because it represents a shift away from blaming the victim. There is no easy way for the conscious mind to control immune response. If I rub up against some poison ivy, the urushiol on the plant's leaves is going to elicit a reaction from my immune system that will result in a rash. I cannot personally prevent that rash by deciding that I will not get a rash. That said, the conscious

---

10. Michael Pollan, *How to Change Your Mind* (New York: Penguin Press, 2018), 313.

mind still has a role: for poison ivy, it begins by memorizing what it looks like and not touching it. I can, and should, name triggers for the condition and avoid these if possible.

Johnson laid out an hypothesis for how stress and trauma can lead to depression: "I don't think someone honestly wakes up depressed, but I also don't think that there needs to be a particularly upsetting event that stands out either. I think some people are more susceptible to depression than others, just like human bodies typically don't like inhaling dust particles but some people are more susceptible to that particular overactive immune response. Looking at this idea that part of the mind has an immune system of some kind, it's easy to see how the slide into 'mental illness'—in particular depression, anxiety, phobias, and addiction. That immune system works by trying to remove anything from the mind that is of discomfort, but it has to work fast because the rest of the mind is doing its normal store-analyse-retrieve, day-to-day business. If someone is horrible to you, the mind first rejects the incident and the person by becoming angry, then it seeks approval from others ('*you* don't think I'm lazy, do you?'), and then perhaps it may seek distraction/ numbness, through food/TV/alcohol/etc. The problems come about when either the mind cannot express anger at all (by prior conditioning) or the person behaves in a way that is, for want of a better word, 'inappropriate,' and escalates the situation, or they're 'needy' and seek approval from any or every source they can, or they have no one to seek approval from, or they have been burned by approval-seeking in the past, and so skip straight to phase three and binge whatever numbness-inducing substance they can. Because all three of those give some kind of reward for the brain (righteousness, approval/comfort, or dopamine/numbness through substance) the brain begins to lock in those paths and encourages that behavior, whilst also labeling the initial experience as upsetting and one to

avoid, so the brain ends up both craving and rejecting the same experience, only the craving is subconscious (and therefore more powerful) and only the rejection is conscious (but not always; sometimes
both are subconscious)."

There is research that suggests that this explanation—that depression may be a reaction to a perceived threat—has some merit, and
may actually be a defense mechanism even if it doesn't feel like it's
doing a body good. It's a subroutine of the body's programming,
reacting according to how it's designed and not controlled by the
conscious mind, just like the reaction to poison ivy, which is a form
of inflammation, one of the basic immune responses in the body.
Inflammation can be triggered by injury, infection, or trauma (physical or mental), among other factors. With poison ivy, some people
encounter the irritant and don't even notice, while others seem to
have no tolerance whatsoever and break out seriously from the
slightest contact. Similarly, not everyone is affected by stress at the
same intensity. There is research into the hypothesis that depression may be a response to inflammation in the body, altering behavior to maximize healing and minimize exposure to others as if
one was recovering from an injury or infection.[11] If that's the case,
then acts of self-sabotage could be seen in the same light as a poison ivy rash: an overreaction, yes, but one that is triggered without
conscious thought.

A normal human approach to the world is the search for ori-
gins, but that's elusive when it comes to depression. While it might
be possible to name the moment when depression began, it was
precipitated by a thousand cuts that weaken resistance and resolve.
Tenpenny searched for a cause for his condition. "I'd always pick

---

11. Vladimir Maletic and Charles Raison, *New Mind-Body Science of Depression*
(New York: W.W. Norton & Company, 2017), 84.

the least changeable circumstance as the cause of my misery, and even if it changed it didn't help, not even temporarily." Not having a clear idea of what causes depression to begin can—like just about anything, when experiencing depression—make the condition worse. If you can't point to that one moment, it's easy to feel guilt or shame, or develop a belief that this is evidence that you are a failure of a person, because *that's how depression rolls.* The truth is that there were likely myriad contributing factors, and no single cause or origin story.

Carl Jung posited that humans put unwelcome aspects of themselves into their psychological "shadow," and Johnson suggested depression might emerge from that same shadow. "Perhaps the shadow really is the higher guardian angel, only we've shoved it so full of pain and anger, and because we only listen to our own self-hatred it has no choice anymore but to speak to us in our own language—one of recrimination and fear. Yes, in some ways, I do think depression is external or it can certainly feel that way, but only because it's all the parts of our soul we've rejected, and in doing so has become powerful enough to manifest in form."

Courtney Weber considers depression "part of my legacy of being a descendant of immigrants." Weber has learned from her own family history that immigrants—even the willing ones—must take steps to cut themselves off from the pain around leaving one's ancestral homeland. Trauma can get passed from one generation to the next. Weber's great-grandmother ended up being a single mother full of "terror and sorrow," she has learned, and impressed upon her daughter the importance of not doing that—living life and rearing a family—alone. "She put fear into her daughter: you must be married, do not take this journey alone. At that time, this meant meeting standards of beauty, and led to an obsession with thinness and a strange relationship with food that has been taught down the line." When one's ancestors are enslaved and shipped to a new life as nothing more than property, one imagines that the potential for trauma being passed down is all the greater.

This is a broader take on the ancestral role of depression than others I spoke to have taken. It's not about whether people in your family tree suffered from the condition so much as whether people in your family tree experienced the sort of trauma that might contribute to suffering from depression. Even if Weber's great-grandmother weathered her pain without experiencing depression, the lessons she learned and handed down had lasting effects for years to come. Add in other lessons from other ancestors, and the convergence can produce conditions conducive for depression to be born.

Anyone can become depressed, Dominguez says. "When you climb the mountain high enough, it's painful. The pain of the knowledge of how difficult it is to fix it all. Sometimes as we are confronted with new revelations, this makes us feel it's hopeless, a Gordian Knot of human culture. The process of learning how things work almost requires there be dark periods."

Considering Tauring's observation that there is no split between body and mind, seeing mental defense mechanisms as an extension of the immune system makes sense. The person is a whole person. The body, the mind, the spirit, the soul and all the parts of it that may have broken away, the many layers or aspects of self, all comprise a whole being. No condition is solely spiritual, or mental, or physical; there is no disease that only affects the mind or only affects the body. Depression doesn't affect everyone in the same way, and some do not experience it at all—despite experiencing emotionally challenging events. Agents that cause disease include microbes and environmental stressors that chip away at the immune system until something bad happens. Every condition takes a toll on every part of the person, albeit in different proportions. The best treatment is the one that addresses the hurt on all levels.

Sarah W. seems also to understand depression as impacting the whole person, saying that depression is "not necessarily a spiritual state. There is brain chemistry and other physical stuff contributing to it. Actual bad stuff happening in life is a factor. Everything has a spiritual aspect, and can at least lead to a spiritual condition like *acedia*."

JOURNAL EXERCISE
Naming the Pain

Set a timer for five minutes.

Definitions can be slippery, but pain is very real. The next time you experience a wave of pain, open your journal and pour out all the words that describe the sensation. Whatever words that rise up, send through the pen onto the page, paying no attention to whether they make logical or grammatical sense or not. Write until all those words and phrases come out.

If you have time remaining, use it to write about the experience using full sentences. The pain may have physical, emotional, mental, and spiritual components. Take note of details such as whether it moves around or remains fixed, if it seems hot or cold, whether it comes in waves or remains steady.

Add three minutes to your timer if you're on a roll, or just stop the timer and keep writing.

This is your experience, your definition of depression. You have named your pain.

two
Depression as Spirit

Depression is a spirit, whether or not it is also other things such as a chemical imbalance, a response to long-term trauma or stress, an immune system reaction, or the result of a difficult loss or change of circumstances. This is not to say that it is a self-created spirit, or an entirely external one, or some sort of amalgam, or something entirely different. My purpose in conceiving of depression as a spirit is that one can *relate* to a spirit. It is in relationship—which is often characterized by struggle—that we can shift dynamics. The experience of depression is static and unchanging, but the relationship with this spirit doesn't have to be.

My experience, and that of others I interviewed for this book, is that depression has a voice, and it's part of the ongoing dialogue that unfolds in our heads. If you have ever talked to yourself, out loud or silently, then you already have at least two aspects involved, the speaker and the listener. When we are feeling conflicted or making a decision, we might have still more voices as part of that internal conversation. The voice of depression is one that sows doubt. If you are concerned about the side effects of medication, the voice of depression amplifies those concerns. If you're worried about people seeing you as weak, depression might suggest that you should feel ashamed of needing assistance, so shut up about it.

If you are mindful of cultural appropriation, this will be used as a wedge to get between you and potential healing through a remedy developed in an indigenous culture, weaving in whatever thoughts about social justice and feelings of guilt might already be there. Depression is in your head. It can turn your worries and fears against you, and it can turn your highest ideals against you as well. It doesn't really matter if it's something that has moved into your head, or was born there, or if it's suppressed parts of the psyche, depression is another voice in the chorus of the mind, albeit one that is trying to lower confidence and self-worth to keep you away from others. That might be a good thing if the goal is to slow a pandemic, perhaps, but the result is this set of seemingly unending feelings of misery that feel similar to grief, just without a beginning or an end.

Since this condition brings a new voice into the conversation, it's not uncommon to think or talk about it as a separate being, like Winston Churchill sometimes did. Churchill once wrote in a letter about a German doctor who treated the condition, saying, "I think this man might be useful to me—if my black dog returns. He seems quite away from me now—it is such a relief. All the colours come back into the picture."[12] Churchill was likely using the phrase "black dog" as a metaphor, but a turn of phrase is not an idle act: when we refer to something as if it has agency, it's because it does have agency, even if we do not recognize this consciously. Some aspects of the self—ones that are not present in the conscious mind—use metaphor as a tool.

Sarah W. has observed that at times, depression seems to push back against positive change. "If part of it can be conceived as a

---

12. Nassir Ghaemi, "Winston Churchill and His 'Black Dog.' Of Greatness," The Conversation, January 23, 2015. https://theconversation.com/winston-churchill-and-his-black-dog-of-greatness-36570.

shadow or unhelpful self, when I have a large breakthrough in my life—mental or otherwise—I will get a bad attack of depression or other issues almost as if something is fighting back, as if its survival is being threatened. It always makes me think one could see it as an actual creature even if it's essentially ourselves, something that doesn't want to be changed." This is something Orion Foxwood has also observed: liminal points in life tend to have higher levels of stress, and that is when depression might move in. Sarah W. added, "I've not engaged as if it's a spirit, but it could be a potentially fruitful line of inquiry."

Depression is a strongly protective spirit, one that smothers as much as a stereotypical, overprotective parent; it only sometimes smothers completely to death but it always stifles the potential to live a fulfilling life. By many measures, my life was stifled by depression: it took me thirty-three years to earn a college degree, my anger and negativity have at times impeded my social relationships, and I'd rather not think about the amount of income I might have earned if my black dog hadn't visited. Anyone who finds the strength to change the dynamics of that relationship deserves respect. I could not have taken the first step without a lot of professional help, but that does not minimize the fact that I *took* that step. The good news that I can share is that the strength to do this appears to build over time, or perhaps it's the wisdom we acquire about this spirit that makes it easier to recognize when it's wormed its way back into the psyche.

Siobhan Johnson sees depression as not the result of an overprotective immune response that can be characterized as a spirit, but a collection of poor coping mechanisms. "We struggle to heal ourselves and end up dismantling any support system in place by pushing people away or punishing ourselves (which lights up those shadow reward pathways again), and because depression comes with a nice serving of self-hatred, we push all of the things we don't like, and some of the ones we do, into our shadow," Johnson said.

"Whilst everyone in the world does that, depressed people do it times ten. Depression really does feel like you're only half a person, and because that subconscious shadow is always stronger anyway, and because we seed it with so much hate, I think it really does *feel* like an external spirit, but I don't think that it really is. I believe that the self is something far weirder than we give it credit for. Essentially, I think we have three main forms: the higher self/guardian angel that floats about in the divine and pings down advice—that which we might call a soul; the second part is the mind, floating about in the underworld, containing higher reasoning, narrative understanding, our own history and experience, the 'monkey brain' if you will; and lastly the body, which is our physical form but also our reptilian brain, that bit of us that's instinctual and animal, containing all our families' and nations' and species' history.

"Spirit and substance are in complex relationship, and the notion that we can perceive a part of ourselves as 'other' is nothing new. There are certainly parts of a human person that are separate beings, or at least were at one point: the mitochondria. Are the different aspects of soul or spirit or self-described in different cosmologies a way that the conscious mind organizes internal relationships, or are we a spiritual amalgam of formerly separate entities, in the same way that mitochondria once existed entirely separate from our distant ancestors?"

I see no conflict with depression being a biological response and also a spirit. In many magical and theological constructs—including the one described by Johnson—the soul is seen as having several parts which are not always in harmony, and seeing humans as a "spiritual amalgam" to me just means that our different parts are in relationship. In particular, it's the conscious mind—the part we most immediately recognize as the self—that has to learn to be in relationship with other levels of self. An immune response that causes more harm than it prevents is certainly not in harmony with the rest of myself. There is no functional difference between the two.

"Long-term depression should be treated as if it were a separate persona," Dominguez agrees, because depression "will attempt to reclaim the territory in the life. We are more colonies than one being." Relating to depression as a spirit doesn't require presuming that the condition comes from within, any more than it means that depression is a visitor from outside the self. It's an acknowledgment that depression acts like it has agency, just like different parts of the soul can act like individual beings with agency. It's acknowledging common experiences of depression, and the language people already often choose to describe it—the language of agency. If it quacks like a duck, it could well be one.

Weber uses the language of personification when discussing depression, but that doesn't mean she'd go so far as to see it as an independent spirit. It's a framing she's familiar with, though; she knows a psychologist who is also a Yoruba priest who sees all mental disorders as spirits, spirits that can be addressed through the techniques of clinical psychology. "I'd love to say depression is a spirit," Weber said, "because then I can work on ridding me of it, but it's more complicated than that. It includes trauma for being bullied and blamed for it, and assault and [bad] relationships, a reason why you're angry and feel that you're bad. What the ancestors experienced stays with us, what they did and what they endured. We also live in a nation of immigrants that lost parts of themselves getting here. This is filling part of ourselves that was lost to our ancestors."

Orion Foxwood said, "Yes, in many kinds of ways," that depression can be seen as a spirit. "It can be parasitic and invasive, [but] not intelligent or evolved ... a larva draining the essence of the person."

The idea reminded Foxwood of the "leaking state" caused by puncturing of the "astral sheath," which can be caused by some kinds of spiritual intrusion, as well as by the evil eye. He believes that if there's a spirit involved, intervention may be called for, but that every case is unique. A parasitic spirit ingrained in the nervous system can cause much damage and needs to be severed, for example, but not every spirit is doing harm even if that appears to be the case. Spirits in the body affect the peripheral nervous system, he said, and "that's how you get visions." Otherworldly, plasmatic beings "will fire neurons," and possession by spirits or deities "can affect the system, as well."

Elementally, depression is the stillness or the aftermath. It has the feeling of the tepid, stagnant water from a ditch. It is the muck that accumulates in the treads of a boot, the clinging fog that obscures sight and confuses sound, the choking embers after the collapse of a hot fire in on itself. As with most beings, depression has within it the qualities of all of the classical elements, albeit in their least energetic form. I do not use "spirit" and "void" as elements as they are in some traditions, but I expect it would not be difficult to find associations with depression for these, as well.

This "line of inquiry" has its own limits. What I wanted from this book is what I wanted from my first blog post about the topic: something to blame. Maybe the reason I can't pinpoint a trigger (or even realize I was having a problem, for much of my life) is because there's an external force, an outside spirit, acting on me. That idea also lets me shift blame for how I feel to that spirit, which then puts me at risk of giving away my power to control those feelings. The allure, when experiencing depression, is to set aside hope, to give up one's own power, to surrender. Seeing depression as a spirit could lead to a feeling of hopelessness, the sense that it's just too difficult to face this challenge, if it's caused by a spirit.

I have chosen a different path. For me, seeing depression as a spirit means I can exorcise it, partner with it, ignore it (at my peril), rage against it, race against it. It is other, which means I can engage and control it in ways that I have not always controlled my own self.

What doesn't work with the conception of depression as spirit is the notion of pure monotheism, by which I mean a single, all-encompassing deity playing all the roles of non-material beings. Monotheism is logically problematic, particularly if the preferred deity is lifted up as being all-loving and all-knowing. Sorry, but the idea that there is a single, endlessly caring god in control of all reality, and that my swimming through the murky tar-rivers of depression is somehow part of that god's plan, doesn't paint a picture of a universe in which I wish to live. No, to me it sounds pretty bleak and hopeless. A strident monotheist might go on to argue that my suffering is *my* choice, not that of this god. I agree that I can influence my relationship with depression through my choices. I understand that there is science that suggests that depression results from some form of immune response, which would technically mean some part of my body or mind is making it happen, the same way the body of someone with Crohn's disease is causing all of *that* pain and damage. That's not the same as saying that depression is my *fault*. Unfortunately, the only options in the monotheist toolkit are to either throw up one's hands and have faith that the machinations of this deity will work out for the best, or to suggest that depression is the result of *not* trusting this deity and thus stepping out of this grand plan and into self-created suffering. I see the animist approach as being much more empowering.

"Slippery" is a word I connect to depression because it tends to evade detection. I also refer to this as "invisibility." When in depression, the condition might be invisible to others that I must interact with, such as coworkers. In the alternative, it might make me withdraw socially and become wholly invisible to others. The worst sort of invisibility, though, is when it remains undetected inside me, influencing my thoughts and behavior. Depression can hide, can act invisible, by making even thinking about it seem unconscionable: "I felt like I didn't deserve to acknowledge the depression," said Weber. "I grew up upper middle class with invested parents. We always had food, and I always knew I was going to college. With my advantages, I don't get to be sad; look at what I had!" However, the gods saw things differently, and when this subject arose, the message Weber received was that "you're not doing anyone favors not addressing this stuff. I pushed a lot of people out of my life. I felt I didn't deserve their attention."

Proving that it wants to survive, depression encourages behaviors that lead to the isolation in which it seems to thrive, and that reduces the chances of treatment. Even as it encourages us to disappear from society and the possibility of being exposed by those who care for us, depression works to avoid detection by its host, as well. If I am inattentive, depression sneaks around and takes its toll and disconnects my mind somewhat from my emotions to numb me. However, emotions come from the body and cannot be stilled, leading to unexpected outbursts of anger, or fear, or sadness. That sort of outburst is a signal that something is wrong. If a spirit ever wanted to keep a human isolated, angry outbursts are a good way to accomplish that.

The word "organism" technically refers to forms of life that have cells; while spirits by definition do not have bodies, they do behave as organisms: they react to stimuli, behave in ways that ensure their continued existence, and adapt to changing circumstances. All of this can be observed in the spirit of depression. For example, the sense of becoming invisible might be a sort of defense mechanism. This reminds me of the protagonist in the Piers Anthony novel

A Spell for Chameleon, Bink, who was aware of possessing a magical talent, but since avoiding notice was part of the magic it was quite difficult to learn more about this power. The longer depression avoids being named, the longer it exists without being confronted by any treatment that might reduce its hold. Other people can sometimes notice evidence of depression first, and part of how depression can be expressed is through withdrawing from social contact. In my own experience, I was resistant to the idea of taking the very medication I needed to help me heal. It seems that people experiencing depression are likely to take steps that prevent depression from being addressed, and to lean into behaviors that make it stronger.

I speculate that not noticing one has depression in the first place is an extension of this trend. Depression does not suffer inspection gladly, by oneself or by other people who are concerned about our well-being. It comes off as irritation, and it leads to isolation: if there's no one around asking questions, then I don't have to think so much about how I am feeling right now.

Whether depression is a single spirit, or if there are individual spirits of depression who are companions to each person experiencing the condition, depression has been with humanity for a very long time. Words like "melancholia" and "acedia" are thousands of years old, and there's no telling how long depression was among humans before anyone named it and wrote that down. It could be a parasite that doesn't drain so much from our species overall to destroy it, but it also might be more like the appendix, a part of ourselves that does not appear to have a helpful role any longer but can do a lot of harm. As a spirit, though, depression is something with which we can relate and negotiate. Some offerings to spirits are made to appease, or turn attention elsewhere. That doesn't require that we understand the motives, either: spirits can cause harm without intending to, and may not even be aware of that fact. Blame can be placed on the relationship, rather than the spirit: we are not on the same page. There is friction between us. That spirit rubs me the wrong way. A relationship may be repaired, or changed, or improved, or sometimes ended, and humans have experience with these challenges. The idea of changing or terminating a spirit is daunting, but a relationship with a spirit may be modified with time and effort.

✥ JOURNAL EXERCISE ❧
Introduce Yourself

Set a timer for nine minutes.

Write a "dear depression" entry in your journal that's a letter of introduction. This is a spirit who has taken up residence in your head, and you want it to know who it's dealing with. Do you threaten it with legal action for unlawful occupancy, ask it to start paying rent, inquire as to whether it's comfortable in there, request that it start helping out with household chores? The tone is entirely up to you, but expect that this might be the beginning of a longer conversation when you decide on the first impression you'd like to convey.

If you find yourself on a roll when the timer goes off, go ahead and keep writing.

three
Your Relationship with Depression

If we consider depression as a spirit, then the symptoms of the condition are the results of that relationship. Based on some of those symptoms, that relationship is often toxic. By seeing it as a relationship, it becomes easy to compare it to other relationships we see all around us.

If you had a friend who, since dating someone new, had started drinking heavily, sleeping all day, and gaining weight, all while struggling to hold down a job or even manage day-to-day activities without an emotional outburst, you might think that the relationship with that new romantic partner has something to do with it. It's no different with depression, except that there's none of the benefits of having a new romantic partner. In either case, you might not get very far just by suggesting that your friend end the relationship; the very idea would be dismissed as preposterous! That's because humans are very effective at getting used to unpleasant circumstances; we are the proverbial frog in the pot of water. We can learn to endure physical pain by tuning it out, such as from cancer or arthritis. However, if someone grasps an arthritic hand too firmly, we recoil from the reminder of that constant suffering. We might just stop shaking or holding hands entirely to avoid that. The same is true of non-physical pain:

we can cover it up and ignore it, but if any attention is brought to it then we are reminded how much it hurts all over again. Dismissing the well-meaning friend who thinks you're in an abusive relationship is a defense mechanism, and avoiding talking about depression is much the same, because thinking about some things makes the hurt come back to the surface. Since depression dwells within a person, no one else is going to observe the relationship directly, but if they probe deeply enough with conversation then you might recoil if they hit a tender spot.

"Since it's poor coping mechanisms that made us depressed in the first place, we struggle to heal ourselves and end up dismantling any support system in place by pushing people away or punishing ourselves," according to Johnson. "And because depression comes with a nice serving of self-hatred, we push all of the things we don't like, and some of the ones we do, into our shadow.... whilst everyone in the world does that, depressed people do it times ten. Depression really does feel like you're only half a person." As mentioned on page 43, Johnson subscribes to a three-part model that includes a higher self, the mind, and the physical body. Depression comes from denying some of that nature and putting it into the shadow, where it can be so thoroughly rejected that it feels like something separate, and from there the conflict—the relationship—that is depression arises.

The relationship's the thing. Poison ivy is not a toxic plant, but it does have a toxic relationship with my skin. The same can be said of this spirit: it only causes harm when it's in relationship with certain people. Let's look at some of the ways this relationship can unfold.

Depression and Money

Money is something humans believe they invented, but that's not exactly true. It's similar to our relationship with electricity, which exists naturally as lightning. Our understanding of meteorology and other sciences did not create electricity, but it did allow us to influence its behavior. Orion Foxwood says that humans can create spirits, and if that's the case then money seems to be just the kind of spirit we could have birthed. Like electricity, though, money is not a tame spirit, even if it was created by human will. It follows rules we do not fully understand, and appears to be equally comfortable with or without a physical form; in fact, money existed virtually long before the first cash was created.[13] I don't know for certain if humans created the spirit of money, or simply created a welcoming home for it when the first coins were minted. I do know that money desires to be spent, and that not spending it can require a force of will—which is why we tend to spend more when we are tired.[14] Restraining that desire can take as much energy as controlling the horses that pull the chariot of the sun, and as Phaeton discovered, sometimes we are simply not strong enough, and the spirits run where they will. If other forces are taxing our reserves, therefore, it's harder to hold onto money.

Depression is an ancient spirit; the condition is mentioned by writers of ancient Greece and Rome, and it probably predates the historical record. Depression is certainly a scourge in the modern world, because it prefers isolation, and technology has made it easy to be isolated even when surrounded by other people.

13. Graeber, David. *Debt: the First 5,000 Years.* Brooklyn: Melville House, 2014,18.
14. Sloan, Carrie. "Why We Spend More When We're Tired (and Other Money Triggers)." The Muse, accessed April 18, 2021. https://www.themuse.com/advice/why-we-spend-more-when-were-tired-and-other-money-triggers.

Depression has evolved alongside humans, the spiritual equivalent of lice. Human lice cannot live anywhere but on human bodies; this relationship is so ancient that there was an evolutionary split between head and clothing lice about around 150,000 years ago.[15] We didn't create lice, but they can't survive without us, and have adapted to our behavior as much as we have to theirs. Depression is the same way, I think: it depends on us to exist at all, even if we didn't create it ourselves.

Whenever someone has a relationship with both money and depression, it can amplify problems with both. Depression saps emotional energy, making it easier to spend without discipline, which can lead to the guilt and self-recrimination that makes a comfortable nest for depression. Spending money makes a person feel good,[16] which is just evidence that money wants to get spent. The short-term relief of spending can send someone into a financial spiral, and facing serious money problems might add enough stress to open the door to depression. More than half of Americans spend more than they earn,[17] and worrying about that can make it worse. People experiencing depression take more time off of work, and the condition may contribute to them losing work altogether; a 2008 study pegged the loss of income in the United States to be $193.2 billion.[18] Basic tasks like managing

15. Parry, Wynne. "Lice Reveal Clues to Human Evolution." Live Science, November 7, 2013. https://www.livescience.com/41028-lice-reveal-clues-to-human-evolution.html.

16. Dahl, Melissa. "Yes, Shopping Can Be Addictive." Elle, January 26, 2017. https://www.elle.com/fashion/shopping/a41845/shopping-dopamine/.

17. AARP Research, "The Three Generations Survey," AARP Research, September 2018. https://doi.org/10.26419/res.00249.001.

18. Insel, Thomas R. "Assessing the Economic Costs of Serious Mental Illness." American Journal of Psychiatry 165, no 6 (June, 2008): 663-665. https://doi.org/10.1176/appi.ajp.2008.08030366.

bills can become overwhelming, even for those who are able to spend less than they earn.

Spending less than what one earns is a fundamental part of managing a relationship with money, but it can be surprisingly difficult to achieve with depression along for the ride. It's not just that one's resolve is weakened and money gets spent more easily; it's also that money is harder to come by. I have struggled with this part especially: my college graduation was delayed by decades, which made it nearly impossible to get a foot in the door and secure a higher-paying job. When I have overcome that barrier, the stress of the work has sometimes meant I lost out on that fat paycheck after a few years because the pressure was taking too great a toll on me. It's been a strain on my marriage, it will have impacts in old age, and there's no social safety net or community values taking this into account. People who lose out on income due to depression are seen as having hard luck or as lacking the hard edge needed to get ahead.

For money and depression alike, we might overestimate our ability to control the relationship if we presume that they do not have agency—which is not the same as sentience. Acknowledging agency is to recognize that we are not entirely in control, and that is a healthy perspective when it's true. Both money and depression will proceed to act whether we are paying attention or not, and they will not ask our leave to do so. Since experiencing depression tends to lower our ability to pay attention, this is an important risk factor to remember. Respecting the agency of others is a good step toward taking control of one's own.

◆§ EXERCISE ≥◆
More Cash, More Control

What you'll need:

- access to your recent bank transactions.
- a way to take some notes.

What you'll do:

- take a look at the activity in your main bank account over the past month.
- find all of the ATM withdrawals and total them up.
- find all the debit card transactions and total them up.
- if you wrote any checks in the past month, total these up.
- add these up and divide by 4.5 to get a rough weekly average.
- at the beginning of the week, withdraw that average amount of cash from your account, and then take your debit card out of your wallet and store it at home.
- commit to spending only cash for the entire week

When we spend cash, it feels different than running a card or writing a check. You will think twice about the money you're about to spend, because money in hand reminds us of what it takes to earn money in the first place.

Depression and Death

There is a relationship between depression and death that is distinct from its relationship with suicide. Depression is sometimes felt as a time when gods are less present, or at least when the gods can be less readily sensed. Two deities that came up as playing against this stereotype are Hela—god of death—and Dionysos, who made at least one round trip into the land of Hades. Ergo, a period of depression might be spiritually closer to those places in which the dead dwell. Medically, the brain's default mode network tends to be hyperactive in anyone who is feeling a lot of distress around the idea of death; the same thing happens in the brain when one is experiencing depression, or is trapped in a loop of self-reflection,[19] which is when I believe depression is building its own cone of power. It's a time when grief and regret can feel amplified; the ancestors are near but the sense of them can be distorted like voices in fog, reduced to mostly raw and unresolved feelings. This is a reminder that the dead are near, even though it's distorted. We feel these terrible things because we are surrounded by ancestors and beloved dead, those forgotten and remembered, of blood and of choice, who have contributed to our identities and who have an interest in our well-being. There are those true voices among the terrible ones that whisper from the cloud of depression, but they can be difficult to discern.

"Depression is a form of death," Ivo Dominguez Jr. said, "feeling like you're separated from the world of the living, puttering around like a hungry ghost in the night, but many parts of us remain alive and well." In a sense, an experience of depression does and should feel like dying, and that can present in a number of different symptoms.

Kari Tauring explained that in Norse tradition, death is tied to darkness, but "darkness is not really seen as evil or bad." It's part of a polarity, and polarities are seen as necessary. "It appears throughout the lore, particularly in Hela," a god who is typically depicted as half living, half dead. "The goddess of the underworld is necessary for rebirth," Tauring said, but is a "frightening figure" who embraces an "awesome mystery; we can't fully conceive of

---

19. Pollan, *How to Change Your Mind*, 353.

transforming death back into life." It's a mystery Tauring sees as common in folk philosophies and traditional theologies.

Death is seen differently in a post-Christian world, according to Tauring: "We are told it's not longer a process, it's a singular event that takes place at a moment in time not of our choosing. The possibility that we will not get out of darkness and back into the light makes it much more scary, as opposed to a natural process of moving one thing to the next, and back again." Indeed, the central tenet of Christianity appears to be that there's just one individual who can make a round trip to the place beyond death.

Just as underworld deities sometimes manifest more easily during a period of depression, the condition is sometimes compared to a journey to the underworld. The deepest throes of depression can feel like living death: the sense that one is disconnected from the life all around, moving in slow motion, ignored or forgotten by others. Such a spiritual journey is sometimes called a *katabasis*, a descent. Any time someone descends into the underworld—via a hospital bed, a shamanic journey, a period of depression—there is a risk of not returning. A person near death due to injury or disease may receive healing to help them. Spirit workers often rely on human and spirit allies to keep them safe. Those who undertake this journey with only depression as a guide, though, often lack any support of their choosing. It can be very difficult to climb back up from the depths without help, but those of us who do return see the world in a different way. The deep darkness of depression is the same as other underworld journeys in how it impacts the psyche, but it's elongated and extended by the slowing effect of depression. Appearing to be moving and thinking more slowly is a medical symptom of depression. My experience is that moments can be extended to near infinity, as if I was approaching the event horizon of a black hole in space. The katabasis with depression extends out like this, and is stretched so thin that one's mind can be present in the world of life while the other parts of the self journey through the underworld.

✦§ JOURNAL EXERCISE ઠ✦
Plan the Journey

Set a timer for thirteen minutes.

Imagine an underworld journey and write about it. If you have undertaken such a journey before as a form of spirit journey, feel free to include imagery from that experience. Otherwise, allow your younger self or subconscious to help you imagine the journey if you were to leave your body even as you write in your journal. Where do you find the entrance to the underworld? Who do you meet on the journey? Does the spirit of depression join you as you descend, or must it stay behind? When you arrive, who greets you? Ask this person if they have any insight to share as to why you have depression in your life. Is it the price for some gifts you have received, a companion passed down through generations of trauma, a quirk of evolution or environment? Let your pen or keyboard be open to the wisdom this person shares. When you've written all you are given, make sure you include at least a sentence or two about your returning to your body.

Suicide

No one wishes for death unless they believe it will be a release from pain. That's true of people whose bodies are racked by advanced cancer and other diseases, and it's also true of people experiencing depression. Anyone who is considering committing suicide, has a specific plan, and is capable of going through with that plan is in danger of dying and should be taken seriously. While the pain of cancer, for example, can also push someone to make a life-ending plan, this is usually done with the help of loved ones or medical providers. If you have a plan to take your own life, and you cannot bring yourself to tell anyone about it, then that's a reason to put those plans on hold. This is a decision you can always make later, but you can never take back. When planning for suicide, embrace procrastination.

Having taken that road to the very brink of death more than once, I can say with confidence that I didn't think that decision through nearly as well as I thought I had. That may be the reason that I had my experience of simulated death, to make me understand that my attempts at suicide in decades past were *in spite of a stupendous fear of my own death.* Fear of death is built right into the operating system of life. When we accept that we are ready to die, we are able to suppress this innate fear because it's got to be better than the alternative. For someone who has been breathing on a ventilator or eating through a tube, this may be true; I fully support the right to die. I imagine that someone in that situation is closer to the spirits of the dead and underworld gods, and these aid in the transition. As depression also brings us closer to the underworld, that kind of powerful energy can contribute to a person's suicidal thoughts and plans.

This is not the only factor that contributes to that most final of outcomes, but any time someone says that they are thinking about suicide it should be taken seriously. When someone shares those thoughts, it's a time to listen without jumping to conclusions. Sharing from that place of vulnerability might be the first step back from the brink of despair.

"Many of my clients are reticent to talk about suicidality because they are afraid of the loss of autonomy and consequences that would come with involuntary detention," Anthony Rella told me. "This threat, and the discomfort some therapists have with holding space for suicidal ideation, is really unfortunate and counterproductive to helping clients with suicidal ideation actually work with the problem. This risk is real but also I think for some a bit overestimated, especially in these times when our hospitalization system is so poorly funded that it is hard to find a bed even for a willing client who desperately needs it.

"When this topic comes up I will often name that this is a risk and may be a barrier for the client, and clarify my responsibilities. Simply having thoughts of suicide is not grounds for detainment. One thing I talk about is the importance of exploring the suicidal parts of us and trying to understand what they are trying to accomplish. When I think of it as 'A part of me wants to die' that is very different from, 'I want to die.' Then we can dialogue with that part and understand its motivation."

I don't regret having attempted suicide. I am speaking from a place of privilege when I say that, the privilege of the living. If I'd succeeded it would have caused a tremendous amount of pain to people who love me, and that's something I did not think through ahead of time. I have no interest in trying again, and I consider that a blessing. I do not know what lies beyond the veil, and I am in no hurry to find out. There will be plenty of time to be an ancestor, if I am fortunate enough to be so named, but my time living as this person is quite limited. This is what's most terrifying about depression: it can make death seem like a reasonable alternative to the pain of living. Anyone who feels that death would be a blessed release should consult with healers to help figure out if this is true. No one should ever make that choice alone. It is always worth considering other options first, and that means talking to other people.

"For the first time in my life the past month I realised how horrible it actually is to want to die, to want to kill yourself," said Siobhan Johnson. "It's always just been a given to me—that it's a normal way to feel... in some ways, it is—humans are fascinated with and desirous of death, of numbness. To love your own mortality is the reason of life and all that, but to spend most of your day fielding impulses to end it all, to force yourself to live for someone else that you love? That's horrible. And it's more horrible in that it's normal."

This is not the underworld journey anyone should be taking. In depression, suicide is just another expression of the self-destruction this condition wreaks. It is a faster route to one's doom, but the slow road is often the surer one to that end. "It can lead to poor self-care, or drug or eating disorders, or people working themselves to death," noted Weber. Pagans seeking an underworld journey should be expecting to return in most cases, but in depression perhaps that's no longer desired. Yearning for death to end pain is understandable, and the pain of depression can be among the worst any person suffers, but it still should not be a terminal condition. My test of whether it's appropriate to plan for one's own death is the ability to share those plans with others and get them to agree. Those are difficult conversations even if it's clear the patient does not have long to live, and that the body's organs are failing. Depression does cause tremendous pain, but the act of admitting to that pain is part of the healing.

"In many cases, the suicidal part is activated because there is some overwhelming pain or stress in the client's life and no other apparent way of resolving the problem," said Rella. "In those cases, we can work on developing strategies for alleviating pain and stress and decreasing the need for suicidal ideation. Suicidal ideation may point to a way that how we live in the world is unworkable, and we could work on helping that painful way of being to die rather than our bodies... Essentially, instead of seeing the suicidal part as this horrible thing that needs to be controlled or eliminated, the goal is to really listen to when and why it shows up, what deeper problem it is trying to solve, and see if we can find solutions that do not require death. One thing that is clear, if the person does choose to die, then they know how the story ends. But if they are willing to stay alive and work with me, we might be able to change the story."

Weber has never had significant suicidal thoughts. "No, I'm afraid of pain," she said. "At one point at around fourteen I wrote in my journal that I just wanted to end it all, but I don't think I really meant that. I wrote it because that's what you're supposed to say. I was exploring the feeling, and decided it's not how I feel. I never had suicide ideation." Weber has been touched by suicide, and "the suffering that results from that choice" has stuck with her.

Many people consider depression and suicide synonymous, but as Weber's anecdote shows, they are not. The relationship between suicide and depression is not the direct line that some people expect it to be. While sixty percent of people who kill themselves have a mood disorder (which includes bipolar disorder as well as major depression and persistent depressive disorder, another form of depression), only about two to three percent of people treated for depression do commit suicide (however, the chances rise for people who have been hospitalize for the condition (four percent), and to six percent of those who have had inpatient treatment after thinking about suicide).[20] (Some thirty percent of people with depression do not receive treatment,[21] and it's believed that half of U.S. adults experience a mood disorder such as depression.)[22] What this means is that while people in depression are certainly more likely to take this action, the vast majority of them still will not.

---

20. "Does Depression Increase the Risk for Suicide?," Department of Health and Human Services.

21. *Psychiatry for the People*, "30 Percent of Depressed People," February 26, 2018.

22. Wanck, *Mind Easing*, 61.

Anthony Rella laid out where the line should be drawn between thinking about suicide, and getting ready to commit the act. "I am legally and ethically bound to recommend hospitalization if the client has a high risk of suicide which includes a plan, the means to execute the plan, and a clear and present desire to act on the plan. As a therapist, my job is to be on the side of the part of the client that wants to live. I believe in autonomy and that each person has the right to do what they wish with their life, and I also believe that if a person has come to me to discuss this, the part of them that wants to live is asking for my help."

Claiming to be suicidal is sometimes the only way a person can get the care that's needed. This is partially because institutional health systems leave no room for human judgment and compassion. Claiming suicidal intent also tends to get more attention than admitting to be depressed because of the slippery nature of that word which has already been discussed. Even so, most people aren't sure how to react if a friend or loved one admits to thinking about ending it all. These reactions tend to be at one extreme or the other: either there will be a push for hospitalization or constant supervision or something similar, or the person confessing to having those thoughts will be dismissed as seeking attention inappropriately.

Rella tackled using threats of suicide as a weapon in a blog post: "A very specific and small group of people use threats of suicide as strategies to guilt their loved ones into staying or giving in during conflicts. Essentially this is a hostage-taking situation, and a strategy of abuse. In this situation, the value of autonomy is an antidote to the threat. If we are all ultimately responsible for our lives and well-being, it is our job to decide whether we wish to live or die. That doesn't mean we don't accept help and support, ask for validation, or ask people to help us find reasons to live. Many of us in the darkest pits of trauma and depression need that help desperately.

Soliciting and accepting help is another form of power and self-responsibility."[23] It's a rare case, though, and jumping to the conclusion that a person is being manipulative is something I try to avoid myself. What's better to provide is an opportunity for the individual to share feelings without judgment. Many people who think about ending their lives never take any steps to create a plan or do the deed, and having a compassionate friend listen to them might be enough. Others will need more help than a friend can provide, but the first step is not to provide advice, it's to listen deeply and help that person feel heard. Only then should permission to offer advice be sought. Any decision to seek professional help will be much more likely to have an effect if the affected person feels like it came from within, and was not coerced.

Adopting the other extreme also has its risks. This perspective—arising perhaps from an abundance of caution—boils down to the idea that depression equals intent to commit suicide. When that's not actually the case (and sometimes, even when it is), this can undermine trust. It's easy enough to withdraw from a social relationship during a period of depression, and having someone from the local mental health agency make a cold call isn't going to improve the situation. Here, again, listening deeply can allow an individual to process and release emotions that could lead to destruction. It also builds rapport and trust, meaning that if a specific plan is developed, you might be told of it before it's too late.

Rella practices in Washington, and described how screening for risk of suicide must go in that state: "Have there been prior attempts? Has anyone in the client's life attempted? Ultimately, the question comes down to, if you leave this room, will you be able to

---

23. Rella, "Pagan Perspectives on Suicide (Part 1)," *A Site of Beautiful Resistance* (blog). https://abeautifulresistance.org/.

keep yourself safe between today and our next session? If the client has a plan, the means, and is unable to make a plan for their own safety, then I will make plain my concerns and recommend they go to the hospital for inpatient treatment. It is important to me to work with the client for as long as it takes to help them feel that it is a decision we are making together rather than one I am forcing them to make. In seven years there have been very, very few times I've called for an involuntary detention. It is an unpleasant responsibility that I do not take lightly. I believe that being transparent with the client about my responsibilities and what I am looking for in some ways equalizes the power and gives them some control over the interaction."

Writing this book took me past my fiftieth birthday, a point in time I would not have reached had I successfully ended my own life. I attempted suicide a handful times in my late teens and early twenties, but I never directly linked those decisions to depression. Rather, being in a depressed state skewed the mix of emotions in such a way that I was able to believe I was approaching this in purely logical manner. What I didn't understand is that there is no such thing as a decision made in absence of emotion. Emotions are more real than thoughts, in that they have a physical manifestation. I believed myself to be someone who largely either didn't have, or completely controlled, my emotions; I was wrong. One can control emotions as well as one can control breathing or blinking, but they cannot be stopped and their existence continues whether or not one is consciously aware of them. Any "rational" decision is always made in an emotional context. Since I didn't understand that fact, I presumed my emotional suppression was actually their absence. I also bought into the idea that logic is separate from emotion. I got that notion from *Star Trek*, despite the fact that Mr. Spock clearly had vast seas of emotion roiling between those pointed ears. It's not that control isn't possible, but assuming one has it can be a dangerous—even deadly—illusion. Therefore, I don't see the depression I've experienced as causing suicide attempts; instead, its existence made it possible for that idea to appear rational.

While I dallied with death as a young adult, only one attempt got the attention of other people. A friend of my roommate's became quite cold to me after that night, eventually becoming openly hostile. When I finally got angry enough to confront him on it, I found out that a close relative had committed suicide, and my attempt reminded him of the feelings of loss and betrayal. We never really spoke again, and I recognized that in my own attempt, I was standing with my foot in the door to the afterlife and that his own unprocessed pain was inflamed with my act. When someone commits suicide in secret like that, the pain is not released so much as redistributed. There are few acts as selfish and destructive as secret suicide, and no one ever contemplates it without depression whispering in their ear first. If you are not willing to run your plans by healers and loved ones in your life, then you are not ready to choose death. Depression can be, in a sense, a terminal illness, but since the cause of death in this case will be suicide, then the way to prevent it from being terminal is not to kill yourself. It may sound overly simplistic, but it's not: depression can be managed in the living, but not the dead.

Rella looked at the question of suicide through the lens of individual agency in that same blog post. "In a pagan context that values self-responsibility and autonomy, however, each person is as empowered to choose their death as they are responsible for their life," Rella wrote. "For those who have lost people to suicide, that tendency toward personalization and blame might depend upon the context of the suicide. We may be willing to offer understanding and empathy for the suicide of those dying of terminal illness or losing their consciousness to dementia. For those who are younger and suffering from mental and emotional distress, however, there is less understanding and often more confusion, shame, and taking the choice personally. When unexpected and painful tragedy arises, our immediate instinct is to reaffirm our sense of control and certainty by forcing the events into our systems of meaning. To really let our spirituality support us and become deeper, we might instead allow ourselves to be present with the pain and confusion and allow it to teach us."

Suicide carries stigma and speaking out about suicide means pushing against the idea that it is not a topic about which one should ever speak. That pressure dovetails sweetly with the dark, quiet places where depression makes its home: Don't talk to anyone. No one cares about how you feel. If they did, wouldn't they be here right now? Of course, you don't talk about it when they visit. They wouldn't understand. No one understands. It's not that you're keeping your plans secret if it's obvious no one cares, right? The voice of depression whispers many things, all while one's energy is being drained, including the energy to do anything but listen to such destructive messages. That's why I believe that the first step anyone should take when having thoughts like these is to find someone with whom to talk. *Humans are a social species*, and it is completely inappropriate to make any end-of-life decisions without consulting with others. If you tell friends or family that you're planning a suicide, they are almost certainly going to try to talk you out of it! If you wish to plan your own death, however, it should not be a lonely death. Those of us who are blessed with the option to choose the time of our own passing should be expected to choose companions to see us part of the way. If you can find no one you love who is willing to attend your death, this is not the best time to die.

The message is that there is something worthwhile in you that you cannot now see in yourself.

Not every decision for suicide is informed by depression, and not every person who experiences depression has an abnormal amount of suicidal thinking. There is certainly a relationship between the two, but in a way I wish people wouldn't choose to link the two concepts because I don't know that it helps. I think it makes the bar for treatment higher, in a way, because we tend to latch onto suicidal thoughts as the only evidence that someone is in crisis. Far more people suffer in depression than ever will try to take their own lives, and each of them is as deserving of love and community as every other person.

Replacing human connection with systems and forms that value blind equality over compassionate equity is a problem that riddles American health care. This is part of why we tend to focus solely on the question of suicide, and I have no doubt it can compound depression. One of my first spiritual teachers knew someone on disability payments who allegedly said, "I am grateful I am not as disabled as they believe I am, or I would never be able to manage the paperwork." Creating barriers to care is not a good look, and it can make getting help seem insurmountable. This is another space that can benefit from more community. Who do you know who is suffering and could use some help figuring out how to get help? If you are experiencing depression, how can you let go of that feeling of futility enough to allow that help? The first step might end up being an emotional outburst of anger or sadness, and there needs to be space for that to occur. The denial of emotion has never solved any problems. When someone expresses very strong emotions like these to me, I want to recoil, but that's because my own emotion is also based in the body, and thus reacts faster than thought. Through mindfulness training I have learned to take a mental step back and ask myself: Is this emotion directed at me, or just being expressed in my presence? I want to allow people to experience and process their emotions if the time and place are safe for that expression. Once the emotions run their course, it's easier to focus on details like paperwork and a self-care regimen.

✑ JOURNAL EXERCISE ✑
Write a Revivicide Note

"Revivicide" is a word I have coined that means, "the act of recommitting to life." You don't need a timer for this exercise.

Open your journal, and write a note explaining all the reasons why you should continue living. It does not matter how insignificant or petty the reasons are, if you think of it, write it down. Do you owe a friend five dollars? Did you finish sorting your socks? Is your mother expecting you to rake the leaves—next fall? Does your dog need to be walked? Will it be hard for your boss to fill your shift? Were you planning to see the next total solar eclipse in your area? Write down all the minor reasons you can imagine, and also write down ones that feel more important, like the friends and family who would miss you if you were gone. You may find it easier to come up with small reasons, and that's okay.

Mark that page of your journal in some way. If there comes a time in the future when don't think you have a reason to live, open it up and take a look.

Drugs and Depression

We all have relationships with certain drugs, but to have a relationship with depression is to alter those relationships. The definition of "drugs" I use here is that they are substances that alter the body chemistry, which is broad enough that it includes even air and food. During periods of depression, it's easy to turn to one drug or another to try to alleviate the symptoms, but this is something of a fool's errand because people in pain often make decisions without intention. No matter what substance one chooses to put into one's body, this should be done with thoughtful intention and in relationship with that substance. Understand what you wish to achieve: Numbness? Happiness? Healing? Alleviation of pain? Avoidance of problems? Solutions to problems? Respect whatever drug you are choosing to take: Acknowledge its spirit, speak your intention, and ask for its aid. Many drugs have strong spirits. Some are single-minded in their purpose (particularly those born in laboratories), but others have both the flexibility and the personality to do many things in partnership with a human. To that end, take care that your stated intention is the one in your heart, because some of these spirits will ignore your words if they contradict your needs. There is good reason why guides are recommended when working with many of these spirits.

There are chemical compounds manufactured in the body, and it's by altering this mix of chemicals that drugs do some of their work. For example, serotonin is a chemical that is specifically targeted by a family of antidepressant medications called serotonin reuptake inhibitors. These SSRIs are intended to maximize the amount of this particular compound floating around inside of us based on the understanding that more serotonin can result in better mood. Nothing is ever quite as simple as that. "Depending on the type of receptor in question and its location, serotonin is liable to make very different things happen—sometimes exciting a neuron to fire, other times inhibiting it. Think of it as a kind of word, the meaning or impact of which can change radically depending on the context or even the placement in a sentence."[24] Even drugs

---

24. Pollan, *How to Change Your Mind*, 292.

that have been deeply studied may have a lesser, greater, or different impact than is expected based on science, because there are many variables not fully understood, including spiritual ones. That is not to say that drugs must be always avoided; all humans have relationships with drugs of one kind or another. Allowing any of these relationships to devolve into dependence is harmful. My main caution is to recognize that every drug has a spirit of its own, and that the use of one spirit to supplant another may yield unexpected results. Science is one of the ways we should analyze our relationship with a drug, but it is not the only way. Do not be afraid to use subtle sensitivity to consider the potential up- and downsides of inviting a drug into your life.

Food

Stress alters diet. Hours before my father's funeral, I found myself unable to keep food down, my stomach in knots and my body rejecting any attempt to untie it. That sense of a "nervous stomach" appears to be one of the ways that the emotions born of the body and the thoughts that emerge in the brain interact. Scientists are even starting to pin down the role of gut bacteria in all of this.[25] Vomiting, diarrhea, and loss of appetite can all be stress taking its toll on a person, but so can reaching for that pint of ice cream that's supposed to serve four, knowing full well that it's going to be a solo adventure. Depression feeds on and creates stress, amplifying changes in diet (such as cravings for comfort foods loaded with sugar and fats) which in turn amplify self-consciousness about body image, which in turn creates more stress and more of the

---

25. Elizabeth Svoboda, "Gut Bacteria's Role in Anxiety and Depression." Discover, October 4, 2020. https://www.discovermagazine.com/mind/gut-bacterias-role-in-anxiety-and-depression-its-not-just-in-your-head.

same food habits. Depression works in cycles, building its own cone of power from the fuel it demands we provide.

Food is one of the most challenging drugs to manage because we need it to live. Poor diet compounds every health problem, including depression, and I don't know any people in depression who are prone to leafy-green-vegetable-eating binges. We tend to crave what gives us a quick bump: fat, sugar, carbohydrates, and salt, which come in many prepackaged forms thanks to the modern food system. That garbage food is also convenient and cheap, meaning that people who work long hours as well as people who have very little money are more likely to be eating poorly in the first place. Poor diet weakens the immune system and emotional defenses, making it that much easier for depression to set up shop and reinforcing those bad decisions to help it take root.

Food can make a difference in healing. Joshua Tenpenny observed to me that "sugar, caffeine, and recreational drugs are not a good diet," but that eating whole and healthy foods resulted in a very different outlook on life. The foods we choose to sharpen our focus or comfort our sadness in the short term can do an excellent job of feeding the depression, too.

A guide for food might come in the form of a nutritionist, or a farmer, or a weight-loss coach, or a therapist to help explore your particular relationship with food, and how to nourish your whole self. Specifics aside, the closer a food is to what it looked like in nature, the healthier it is probably going to be for the human eating it. Separating the relationship of food from emotions is not easy, and I am not sure it's even possible to do this entirely. To learn to be mindful about food choices, on the other hand, is absolutely something anyone can achieve and something toward which everyone should strive.

Prescription Medications

Medications to manage depression can be controversial. I was completely opposed to taking a psychiatric medication, but I was not given a choice. For me, at that time, it was absolutely the best thing that could have happened, because healing was not happening and I was in crisis. I had lost a good deal of my emotional range until the fluoxetine was working in my system, and then I had all of my feelings back. I was able to smile and laugh, as well as rage and cry. I'd thought that these pills were going turn me into some kind of happiness zombie, but that was not my experience at all. I was blessed by getting the correct prescription for my needs. Of all the possible side effects, all I had to endure was some cotton mouth. The drug did everything promised in the marketing, and nothing that I'd feared might happen.

I was blessed in my experience. It's not nearly that easy for everyone. Psychiatric medications are complicated, and finding the right fit is a tricky business. My mother struggled with this, having to have her antidepressant prescription changed several times over the course of her life. That feeling of uncertainty, the question of side effects, and worries about things like loss of self and chemical dependence are among the many reasons someone might be hesitant to try a psychiatric medication, and that doesn't touch on the cost and the insurance paperwork. Psychiatrist Bick Wanck writes about the need for doctors to be cautious in prescribing these powerful drugs, saying that it should be reserved for a time when it's obvious that "the use of medicine to reduce the intensity of the symptoms like panic or despair that could otherwise overwhelm your capacity to heal" is the best choice. "Medicine can be a lifesaver and a lifestyle saver when used correctly."[26]

---

26. Bick Wanck, *Mind Easing* (Deerfield Beach, Florida: Health Communications, Inc., 2019) 5.

Even psychiatrists who are cautious in dispensing medications might not know what questions to ask of the pagan patient. People with psychic sensitivity sometimes report a dulling in that area, which can be alarming to people who value those esoteric experiences. Orion Foxwood has spoken with people who lost the voices of beneficent spirits upon switching medications, people who cannot bear to have that sensitivity cut off at any cost. Fortunately Raven Kaldera assured me that this condition tends to be temporary "when it's a good med for your head," with suppressed sensitivity returning over a period of months. Having psychic sensitivity may make it easier to identify the best medication more quickly, then, but the more frankly and openly you can talk with your provider the easier it will be to find the one that clicks for you.

"In my work as a mental health therapist, I've noticed that sometimes people experience very encouraging initial results with medications, only to have those taper off and become more moderate as the body adjusts," writes Anthony Rella in a blog post. "This is particularly painful for those who see a glimpse of a life that the sufferer couldn't have imagined before, and allow themselves to hope, only to feel crushed when things even out."

Whether or not to use prescription medication should be a choice. It was not for me. I had given up some of my autonomy when I elected to take other drugs off-label and had to be removed from my home in a restraining stretcher. If I had gotten the help I needed earlier I might have been given the opportunity to make that choice for myself. If you want to remain fully in control of your own life choices, it's essential to find a way to get help before someone in authority takes that right away. Otherwise, you're trusting that your gods, or spirits, or guiding light is going to force good choices on you when you're not allowed to make any for yourself. That's how it worked out for me, but I wouldn't recommend it.

The guide for a prescription medication should a psychiatrist or someone else trained to dispense medications that affect the brain. Changes can come on quickly or slowly, but because of the nature of the brain, it's easy to miss them, just like it's easy to overlook depression itself. This is an especially good time to keep a log of your moods on paper or electronically. Set alarms or otherwise make a point to make a note of how you're feeling two or three times a day. When that alarm sounds, write down the first mood that comes to mind and don't second-guess it. If there are people in your life that you trust, ask them to mark any changes in your behavior, as well. A medical doctor can't get nearly as much information from a brief consultation as from these data collected between visits. More importantly, if you experience a serious side effect, tracking data may help you recognize it more quickly and contact the doctor right away.

These kinds of medications are incredibly powerful, and their spirits must be harnessed to effect the best change. This is done by including therapy along with the pills. I've had medication without therapy, and I do not find it to be nearly as effective as the pairing. The psychiatrist remains the guide, but in this case there should also be a companion in the form of a therapist or counselor.

Given the multiple problems with health care in the early twenty-first century, I have no doubt that there are people who are able to get antidepressants on the black market more easily than they can from a doctor. Late in the period when I was taking an antidepressant, I got out of the habit of taking it for a few days and emotionally crashed in a way that terrified me. It wasn't the return of symptoms, per se, that brought me up short, but the utter loss of control I started to feel, which reminded me of times when I had even less control and started me on a cycle of fear and anxiety. I was able to get it sorted because I was still safely within the bubble of health care that covers some Americans, but far from all. My heart goes out to anyone who is dependent on a daily medication to live, but is not certain how the next dose will be obtained.

Still, I cannot recommend that anyone take a psychoactive medication without proper supervision. Even trained professionals don't always know what is going to happen to a person taking one of these drugs, and close monitoring of the effects is necessary to ensure that the patient is not put into more danger, rather than less. There are alternatives for people who can't pay for a doctor, but they often take some homework. There is no shame in applying for help through a social welfare program, for one thing. I resisted that myself because I was brought up to be self-sufficient, promulgating American values that tend to undermine community and foster depression. My resistance to obtaining a medicaid card melted away when I got some advice from my father, the very source of those values: "You should apply," he said. "I've been paying into the system all my life, and it's about time I got something back." There's a bit to unpack there, but what I heard is what I have repeated to others many times since: welfare programs exist because people in need deserve to be helped. There should be no exceptions.

I have also found other options at different points in my life, when I lived without that comfortable safety net of medical insurance. I found a clinic not far from my home where therapy was priced on a sliding scale, and medications came in the form of sample packs. This is one of the ways that the invisible hand of the prescription drug market moves: doctors are given copious free samples of these medications. The sinister undertone is that of a drug dealer saying, "The first taste is free," and then charging once you're hooked. Regardless of the intent, the reality is that doctors use these samples to help people who can't afford to buy it for themselves. Ask the doctor if there are any samples available because cost is a barrier.

The bottom line is that anyone who feels they need a prescription medication for depression should not be taking it without a medical professional's supervision. I recognize that the barriers to appropriate health care are real and daunting for far too many people. What's worse is that experiencing depression can make even ordinary tasks seem daunting; a byzantine bureaucracy is enough to turn away even people that have the financial resources to get the care they need. Advocacy and magic to bring justice to health care is an ongoing need, but not one that is the focus of this book. Additionally, none of this changes the fact that these are dangerous chemicals that can cause harm as easily as they can repair it.

Tobacco

In an ideal world, tobacco would be consistently honored as a sacred plant with a powerful spirit, one that can promote healing of body, mind, spirit, and community. My own relationship with tobacco is much more common than the one I just described: I smoked cigarettes for 15 years. Back when tobacco was widely advertised, the "flavor" was often part of the marketing, but it wasn't the flavor that I found appealing. Instead, I was drawn to the burning sensation as I inhaled, and the curious quiver of my throat as I automatically stifled the cough—perhaps that's what the marketers meant when they talked about "flavor." What made it difficult for me to quit, though, was the social aspect. A smoke break is a time to make friends, because asking a stranger for a light is an easy way to strike up a conversation. Even with all of the misuse and abuse this spirit has endured for the sake of profit, tobacco's essential power still comes through.

Few spirits that we encounter in the material world have such power. I am deeply saddened by the poor way it has been treated. It is possible that tobacco is finally falling out of favor as a product.

If this occurs, I hope that it's the first step toward healing our relationship with what should be a beneficent spirit.

I do not believe it is possible to form a healthy relationship with this spirit if you have ever smoked tobacco in a non-sacred context. Given how terribly this spirit has been treated by most humans encountering it, I would not recommend seeking it out at all to obtain healing. Those who seek a guide to meet tobacco should instead be prepared to help this spirit heal from this terrible harm, rather than the other way around.

Herbal Remedies and Supplements

Witches and other pagans may choose to turn to herbs to help with many health issues, and depression is no exception. Whether one is skilled at foraging, an intentional gardener, or purchases herbs at the local esoteric shop or health food store, these plant allies can have powerful effects. Depending on how they are obtained, their form can be anything from the original plant to a processed collection of chemicals packed into a pill, blurring the line between an herb and a supplement. They are worth discussing together because they have certain characteristics in common. Herbs and supplements fit well into the broader definition of "drugs" that I am using here, but many people don't consider them as such because they are often only lightly regulated.

If herbs didn't have the potential for a profound impact, why would anyone take them? They are most certainly drugs, albeit drugs that have been deemed mild enough that they don't need much regulation, similar to aspirin or cough syrup. Herbs and supplements can interact with other drugs, which is why it's important to advise your doctor or pharmacist about the ones you're taking. The intended effects and side effects of herbs and supplements tend to build up over a period of time, meaning that it can be tricky to identify how well they are working. As with prescription medication, keeping a mood log might be helpful when taking a supplement or herb for depression, and no one should be eating any unfamiliar plant without doing some research first. Some plants can kill you, and going out harvesting without a teacher to help you identify what's what might be dangerous for that reason.

There are a couple of herbs and one supplement that I take, and I have found that my need for them varies with the seasons. It took me a number of years to find the best flow for me, and what's really helped is to form a relationship with these spirits to understand how best they can teach me. The results of using any kind of herb or supplement will vary with the quality of the product, the chemistry of the body into which it is taken, and the nature of the relationship the user has established with that spirit. While one can certainly achieve a variety of biochemical effects by munching on a leaf or flower or swallowing a few capsules with water, I wouldn't be an animist if I didn't think that these benefits can't be improved by thoughtful attention, intention, and gratitude.

I cannot recommend any herb or supplement, but I will recount the ones that I have personally found effective, which are:

- **Vitamin D,** which has been discovered to have a wide variety of health benefits. I think of it as liquid sunlight, gift of Apollon, because our skin can and will produce it when exposed to the sun. Unfortunately many of us don't get enough light to generate enough of this substance on our own. We cover ourselves in chemicals out of fear that the rays of the sun will cause cancer, or are trapped inside even during pleasant weather by our obligations.

- **St. John's Wort,** the poster child for holistic depression help. In addition to tracking mood while using this, be aware that it can make some people sensitive to bright light. That might be a good reason to reduce or eliminate its usage, especially if you're not also seeing improvements in mood.

- **Plum flower extract,** an Asian herbal supplement sometimes marketed as "free and easy wanderer." The naturopath who recommended this one to me advised me to take it whenever I—or a family member—noticed my mood was turning sour. Over time I have found that I am more prone to dark moods during the dark time of year, and I take some daily during the winter.

Magicians have even more possibilities because herbs that should not be consumed might be well-suited to becoming spell components. There are many resources available for learning how to tap into the magical potential of plants. Even medical and scientific works often have information about the symbolism of plants, but in the United States I find that books on conjure are particularly helpful because the authors are familiar with the herbs that are already growing here, rather than depending on exotic imports that far too often become invasive intruders. I also use a phone application that allows me to identify an unfamiliar plant by taking its picture. It remains important to spend some time sitting with any unfamiliar plant and becoming familiar with its spirit before using it in magic, even if the end goal is not to put it inside the body.

Herbs and supplements do not have a ready-made guide; the village herbalist is unfortunately not a common sight. It's important to do research, to get to know the spirits involved, and to seek advice from knowledgeable people whenever possible. Remember, whenever looking for answers online, it's important to understand the quality of the source, and a good way to start that process is to see how many other sources are cited on a particular web page. If you choose to take an herb or supplement to help manage depression, keep a mood log and make a note of what you're taking.

Self-Guided Drug Use

This is a behavior, rather than a group of substances, but it's a behavior that captures that large swath of drugs that aren't part of most formal treatment plans. Anyone who makes a decision to use a drug because it mitigates the effects of depression, but does not have a guide in that process, is engaging in this behavior. That includes the use of any prescription medication outside of a doctor's supervision, the use of drugs that are largely or wholly illegal to purchase or use (including alcohol), as well as most uses of herbal supplements and some uses of food. As I have discussed most of these categories already, I shall focus on the unsupervised use of legal and illegal drugs in this section.

This includes illegal recreational drugs, those synthesized chemicals and plant products that have been deemed so dangerous that they have no therapeutic purpose, as well as alcohol, which has been given a legitimate purpose in western society but is one of the most dangerous drugs humanity has ever produced. Even this is a fuzzy category; as I write this, one of these drugs—cannabis—exists in a legal liminal space in the United States, with its use for medical or even recreational purposes allowed in some states even while federal law lists it among the most irredeemable of substances.

Depression causes pain in many people, and that pain can be both mental and physical. Chronic pain can make one vulnerable to depression, and depression can result in chronic pain. It's another way that the dark cone of power of depression is raised. People who experience chronic pain will try to dull or eliminate that pain in any way they can. At some point, a bottle of wine or a packed bong or a pipe might seem like the best alternative. Many of these drugs are quite effective in dulling physical and emotional pain in the short term. Heroin was once prescribed by doctors, suggesting that they saw some healing value in it before they decided that its addictive properties are far too dangerous. Alcohol is another depressant that can provide relief from pain but, like heroin, can lead to much more serious problems if a dependency develops. The idea of using a depressant to address depression might seem fraught with peril from a purely logical standpoint, but like attracts like, and it's entirely in the character of the spirit of depression to encourage the use of a drug that could make things worse in the long run.

Self-medication carries risks because it is often done without clear intent. Feeling pain, we turn to a substance that we have learned might mitigate that pain. Without intent, we are less likely to engage with the spirit of the drug, and more likely to be ignorant of—or simply ignore—the possible drawbacks of using that substance. There is no plan but to escape pain.

Let's be clear: depression is painful. People who have felt grief and sadness so powerful it feels paralyzing might have a glimpse of the emotional dimension of that pain, but depression can also result in pain in the body, from generalized aches to back problems to stomach cramps and beyond. Pain shortens patience and emotional fuses, making someone a lot less pleasant company, and taking a drug to alleviate that pain can thus make that individual into better company. Therefore, there is often positive reinforcement for using some substance to become more acceptable in society. If the substance in question becomes less effective, as most of them do when used indiscriminately, then the quest for something with more punch might begin. Too frequently, that quest leads the seeker to something to which that person becomes addicted.

Healing does not stem from addiction. It's another of those feed-back cycles that helps build the dark cone of power for depression.

There are people who can say that their self-medication choices have contributed to healing; it would be disingenuous for me to claim that this is not the case. The main problem is that people experiencing depression are not approaching these substances with intention, or in any systematic way. If one does not respect the spirit with whom one is communing, and also is not carefully monitoring results to see which substance and at what dosage benefits are felt, then the only way anything positive is likely to happen is under the protection of the gods. I trust in the gods, but I also recognize that the gods gave us the ability to help ourselves and help each other as the first lines of protection. If those are ignored, the best one can hope for is not to do harm to oneself with these haphazard experiments.

Alcohol is not my drug of choice. Not only am I quite prone to becoming hung over, I have a family history of abuse and I do not always know my limit. It only took me a few experiences of having friends tell me how I'd behaved and wondering if they were making things up since I had completely blacked out to convince me that I didn't want to be the known as that person. Alcohol results in relaxation of the body and depression of inhibitions, which can feel like euphoria and self-confidence. That's enough to ease the pain of depression for a while, but by the time those benefits wear off, dependency may have set in. There are no laboratory tests to determine if a person is prone to alcoholism, which means that choosing to drink the stuff is to assume the risk of addiction. There are self-assessments that a person can use to identify if drinking alcohol has become a problem, however. Since we cannot know the risk of addiction until after we've used this drug, I recommend proceeding with caution. Alcohol is a depressant, and anyone who is prone to experiencing depression should assume that alcohol will eventually multiply the harm.

Cannabis, on the other hand, has appeared to be a much gentler companion to me, at least on the surface of our relationship. This plant has a powerful spirit, one that I have seen turn some people into balls of quaking fear and paranoia, but it resonates with me. That isn't to say that I have always approached cannabis mindfully and with intention, though. I grew up during the height of cannabis prohibition and I feared admitting to my spiritual teachers that I had tried it, much less ask them for advice about it. Nevertheless, cannabis for me became an ally during my most difficult period of depression; I used it only at the new and full moons for about six months after my hospitalization and I believe it helped me to synthesize what I was learning from my medication fluoxetine.

Cannabis is an amplifier, one that helped me improve my sensitivity to the emotional range that opened up for me while on that prescription medication. During that period I learned to recognize my emotions more effectively than I had before, including the ones that had felt absent in my premedicated depression. That in turn allowed me to eventually stop taking the pills altogether. Santa Maria—the name for this spirit that has emerged from the Santo Daime tradition in Brazil—is not a *tame* spirit, and will amplify what needs to be noticed, if it's used without intent. Sometimes for me that's the depression itself. That's actually as horrible as it sounds, bringing with it more mental paralysis, physical pain, dark thoughts, and antisocial behavior than I might normally experience during depression alone. It's also beneficial, for two reasons. First, I can sometimes detect the presence of depression sooner if it's amplified by Santa Maria. Second, "sometimes it's okay to be sad," as Orion Foxwood told me, and leaning into that darkness has soccasionally led me to important revelations about myself. It's an intentional approach, but a painful one. Sometimes the gods and spirits smile upon us despite ourselves, or give us what we need over what we desire. Santa Maria is a healing spirit, but be prepared to pay a price for that healing. If Santa Maria is used with intention, the price will at least be negotiated up front.

To use any prescription medication outside of doctor supervision is fraught with peril. Even over-the-counter drugs like aspirin can harm or kill, and prescription drugs are often much more powerful. Among these are opiates, which can do a bang-up job numbing pain, at least for a short time, but often do more harm than good even when there is a doctor involved. I believe that the spirit of the poppy—which gives us all opiates (drugs like morphine and heroin) and lives also in opioids (synthesized drugs using the same molecular structure)—is far too strong for human contact and should be avoided entirely. There is no safe way to seek the help of this spirit, just as there is no safe way for a mortal to look upon the true form of a god. We are simply too frail, and we must choose a different path.

I refer to these as self-guided drugs because there is often no intention to use any help in connecting with these spirits. In truth, the guide we occasionally have is a god, or the spirit of the substance itself. There is no question that many people choose to medicate themselves without any sort of *human* guide. Unfortunately, the subtle voices of gods and other spirits can be drowned out by the destructive ones we hear during periods of depression. I think the depiction of what goes on in a human mind that resonates best with me is in a scene late in the movie *Matrix Reloaded*, where the protagonist is talking to the architect of that world, who stands in front of a wall of television screens depicting the protagonist.

Each of them reacts differently as the conversation progresses, much like the many voices within each of us. The voice of depression is a particularly compelling and especially negative voice, and it draws the attention easily. That's the main downside to trusting oneself as guide, because a guide rightly should be outside of the experience. It takes a lot more discernment to name of the voice of a god than the voice of a human being in the same room. Without clear guidance, it is much more difficult to safely navigate the potential legal and health risks of using a drug.

✦§ EXERCISE §✦
Taking a Break

The greatest danger of self-guided drug use is the inability to recognize when use becomes abuse. There is a bidirectional relationship between experiencing depression and substance dependence. Drinking alcohol might lift the mood, for example, but missing work due to intoxication or withdrawal can make one even more susceptible to depression. If your intention in using a drug is to avoid pain—or if you don't know your intention at all—this exercise is for you.

What you'll need:

- a calendar or other way to determine the moon phase.
- a glass of water.
- a small amount of each of the drugs you're using without a guide.
- a bucket filled with soil or sand (optional).
- small garbage bag (optional).
- a bowl.
- your journal (optional).

What you'll do:

1. Identify the next full moon. You will begin at the moment of the full moon, or as soon afterwards as you can. The moon must be waning.

2. Place the bowl before you, and set the water within reach.

3. Look at the moon with your eyes or in your mind's eye, and say: "Mistress of the rising tides, I bring you an offering. May it not be the last one I make to you."

4. Pour a small amount of water into the bowl—just a quick tip of the container.

5. Say: "Beautiful moon, my offering is unconditional, but I also beg a boon. If you will, take these spirits into your care, and carry them away on the tide of emotion. You whose face is ever-changing, help me to see my face uncovered."

6. Place the substances into the bowl, one by one. Say, "Strong spirits, I wish to stand apart for a time to ensure that you have not overwhelmed me, for my own spirit is not always as strong as you."

7. Add some more water and say, "By your will and mine, let this be done."

8. Disposal of the offerings: If you only added natural substances such as plants to the bowl, then find a storm drain and pour it out nearby. If it includes prescription medications or other refined chemicals, that way will bring harm to the environment. Instead, mix what's in the bowl into the sand or soil in the bucket, pour that mixture into the garbage bag, and dispose of as you would trash that cannot be recycled.

9. Each night during the waning moon, make an offering of water to the moon. If you like, journal about your experience of not using these drugs today.

10. When the new moon arrives, make another offering of water to the moon, and ask for a sign if and when you should resume using each of the substances.

11. If you are unable to complete this process for any reason, seek help from a professional to assess whether you have become dependent or addicted to any of these drugs.

Entheogens

There is a fascinating amount of research being done into the use of psychedelics to treat depression and other conditions. There is also some amount of history of psychedelics being used in religious ceremonies for the purposes of enlightenment and healing. In *How to Change Your Mind*, Michael Pollan explores both the science and spirituality that is informing how psychedelics are being used in the twenty-first century. These are drugs that are largely illegal in the United States—with even research being very restricted—making Pollan's work remarkable in its depth. Whether it's a manufactured chemical like lysergic acid or a plant spirit such as psylocybin or ayahuasca, psychedelics can lead to what's essentially a rewiring of thoughts, breaking down mental patterns that feed into the negative cycles that perpetuate the relationship with depression.

"I do not use entheogens in my shamanic work—that one's not my path—and I would be very wary of using them on someone whose brain chemistry and general psyche may be already fragile," shaman Raven Kaldera told me. "Entheogens are not for mentally fragile people because they can blow things up. Meditation and pranayama breathing, on the other hand, may be helpful. In general, you need gentle techniques for depressive people. Emotionally intense treatments can make them withdraw further."

That caution by Kaldera is an important one. I do not have the expertise or the authority to recommend that anyone use a psychedelic, but I also know that I am not the only pagan who considers them entheogens, substances that are used in a spiritual context to bring about understanding or healing. I have had two profound religious experiences that arose from the use of entheogens that have been beneficial in my own healing journey. In the earlier case, I was processing some extremely dark emotions; it culminated with me being confronted by Ares, who reminded me that I should not ignore the gods, and then set me on the path of Hellenic polytheism. The more recent experience allowed me to see a visual representation of my depression as a physical object, from which I completely recoiled; the wisdom I received led me to create a depression totem according to the process I have described elsewhere in this book.

Nevertheless, this is a line of research that is showing promise. An opinion piece in the *Guardian* laid out some of how psychedelic treatment seems to differ from using serotonin reuptake inhibitors (SSRIs), which are a common family of antidepressant drugs. "Where SSRIs are concerned, their antidepressant action seems to rely on a moderation of the stress response—but it is a palliative rather than curative action, which requires having the chemical in the body for several months or longer. Psychedelic therapy is a much more comprehensive treatment package. It entails a small number of psychologically supported dosing sessions, flanked by assessment, preparation, and integration (talking through one's experience afterwards). Psychedelics appear to increase brain 'plasticity' which, broadly speaking, implies an accelerated ability to change. The impact of successful psychedelic therapy is often one of revelation or epiphany. This is very different from people's descriptions of the effects of SSRIs, where a contrasting feeling of being emotionally muted is not uncommon."[27] A study of psilocybin showed that the chemical found in certain mushrooms "was efficacious in producing large, rapid, and sustained antidepressant effects in patients with major depressive disorder."[28] That study involved just twenty-four participants, but while that number is relatively small it's one of the most rigorous on the use of a psychedelic therapeutically that's been published as of this writing, and suggested that far more people might benefit from this approach than by taking prescription antidepressants. An important aspect of this early research is that there is a system in place to help address Kaldera's concern. People weren't just handed psychedelic mushrooms and told to check back in later; all the participants had a guide.

Guides for taking these journeys are essential; I borrowed the very concept from the psychonaut community, the people who seek out and study these experiences. Do not approach these or any powerful, unfamiliar spirits without someone able to make the introduction. Recognize that a bad relationship with any of them can result in harm to mind and spirit, body and soul. Acknowledge whatever legal risks are involved before deciding to engage in this sort of work.

---

27. Carhart-Harris, Robin. "We can no longer ignore the potential of psychedelic drugs to treat depression." *Guardian*, June 8, 2020. https://www.theguardian.com/commentisfree/2020/jun/08/psychedelic-drugs-treat-depression.

28. Davis, AK, Barrett, FS, May, DG, et al. "Effects of Psilocybin-Assisted Therapy on Major Depressive Disorder: a Randomized Clinical Trial." JAMA Psychiatry. Published online November 04, 2020. doi:10.1001/jamapsychiatry.2020.3285.

Thankfully, the wisdom and training of these guides is maturing, in part because the societal perceptions are changing. "Many of these guides are credentialed therapists," writes Pollan, and "by doing this work they are risking not only their freedom, but also their professional licenses. I met one who was a physician and heard about another. Some are religious professionals—rabbis and ministers of various denominations, a few call themselves shamans, one described himself as a druid."[29] Advancing science, along with recognition of traditional wisdom, is helping this process and making it more and more possible to tap into the healing gifts of these spirits. Anyone who is interested in learning more should probably start by asking a psychiatrist about that emerging research. There is no area of healing for which "informed consent" is more important, given the complex web of legal, medical, and spiritual consequences of setting out on this path.

One thing about which I cannot be too clear: I am a priest, not a doctor. My responsibility in a sacred context is to recognize when someone needs to be referred to a medical or mental health professional. Furthermore, every journey with depression is informed by one's health and one's history, meaning that anything written in this book probably needs to be tailored to that unique set of variables. One of the ways to embrace community is to seek the opinions of human beings who know something about you, or with whom you are willing to share. There is no one person who has all the answers, but in community every problem is easier to solve and every burden is easier to bear.

---

29. Pollan, *How to Change your Mind*, 223-4.

✦§ EXERCISE ⸎✦
Change Your Own Mind

A profound effect of psychedelic entheogens is how they alter our neural connections, allowing our thoughts to travel down paths we may have forgotten. If you want a taste of retraining your brain without help, take a day and try only using your non-dominant hand. That discomfort you feel lets you get a glimpse of how deep the mental channels are in your own brain.

The Isolating Influence of Depression

When I was first visited by the black dog, it completely crushed me under its weight. It was as if I existed in a burning fog that felt like it would suffocate me—or flatten me by mass alone—long before it ever turned me to ash. (I will not apologize for mixing metaphors in my descriptions of depression, because depression is a spirit the effects of which transcend a single word picture.) That increasing drain on my reserves left me vulnerable to the slightest emotional upset, and I quietly attempted suicide a handful of times in my late teens and early twenties. One of the possible outcomes of a journey with depression is death, and not necessarily through outright suicide. Lack of concentration always makes driving more dangerous, as can lack of sleep. Lack of motivation can dispel exercise routines and healthy eating habits. There's a host of substances people with depression put into their bodies to influence their experience, and all of these carry health risks. There are endless ways to take one's own life little by little without it carrying the stigma of suicide. For me, the pain was so raw that at times suicide felt like the only solution. Not every person with depression has that extreme experience, just as not every suicide victim also has depression. Yearning for death is no longer part of my own experience. It is the most immediately dangerous expression of depression, but depression can be profoundly destructive even without thoughts of ending it all.

Social invisibility was one of the first symptoms of depression I recognized in myself, long before I named depression itself as the cause. The emotional pain I endured during periods of depression felt like a physical ache in my chest, a weight that was palpable and unceasing, yet left no physical mark. This seemed right to me, and on some level I understood that emotions come from the body to the mind, and that pain is used to warn when any part of the body's systems—including emotions—is off balance. It was pain every bit as real as being punched, but since it had no physical cause I had no words to discuss it. My pain in those moments reminds me best of the myth of Meleager, the Hellenic hero who was fated to live only as long as a particular log lasted in a fire; when that brand, long safeguarded, was cast back into the flames Meleager died along with it. The clutching of my heart by an unseen force during some periods of depression is similar to what I imagine Meleager must have felt. It is an invisible pain, and in time it made me feel invisible, too. I felt like I was walking around wounded, but no one could see that anything was wrong. My tongue felt frozen against speaking about it, as if I'd been targeted by a spell. In time, I began feeling like people couldn't see when anything was *right*, either. People just stopped seeing me altogether. It may have even alleviated my anxiety about getting bullied, but I was swimming in a dark pool of misery by then and just didn't notice.

Another tendency in depression that reminds me of invisibility is also a bit like tunnel vision. Human brains are designed to see what they expect to see, discarding most of the information received from the eyes in order to make a narrative we can understand. The reason why psychedelics cause hallucinations is because that filtering is turned off completely, and it's possible that when people see a non-physical being, it's because their brains aren't filtering out information that many other people are simply ignoring. The filters we use during a period of depression, however, have us overlooking beauty and joy. Nimue Brown described that kind of experience, writing, "As for connecting with nature—I walk for transport, so unless I am bodily ill, it's rare that I don't go out for some reason during a day. My route to town is twenty minutes—various routes are available to me, I usually see a lot of wildlife. When I'm depressed, I see less, I don't feel it the same way, I'm not as alert or as open so I may not notice the buzzard spiraling overhead or the flash of a kingfisher. Depression trashes my focus and shuts me into myself."

This sort of tunnel vision is incredibly familiar to me, and I expect I'm not alone in that. During depression, one can easily feel like every moment of life is pain and misery, but that's not actually true. In the next part of this book, I recommend tracking one's mood. Anyone who dutifully keeps a log of one's mood throughout the day will discover that there is indeed happiness happening, but it's forgotten as soon as it's over. People who describe the world as being less full of vibrancy and color are expressing this in a different way, as are people like Nimue Brown, who become a bit more oblivious to things that spark joy in nature. The world has changed not one whit, but due to a shift in focus our ability to notice and retain broad swaths of experience fades away.

Courtney Weber was "bullied hard from third to ninth grade," and recalls that "there was no safe place for me where people left me alone." Complaining about bullying at school sometimes got Weber support, but sometimes she was instead accused of drawing attention to herself. She also recalls that "my dad showed love by picking on me, and made fun of me for saying that people made fun of me." The result was that she adapted: "I aligned myself with safe things, what others liked." In short, protective coloration was activated, making Weber less noticeable.

Being a target for bullying is an especially easy way to wear away what defenses we might have, because it's not just the bullying, is it? There's also the frustration expressed by the people who we turn to for help, because no one's really come up with an effective way to stop bullying. Maybe outright violence will do it sometimes, but considering that bullying is a form of violence, that could easily blow up and make things worse instead. If the bullying alone doesn't succeed in making someone feel isolated and cut off from community, the lack of support often can seal the deal. Given that depression tends to make people want to withdraw from others, bullying creates the ideal environment to ensure it thrives.

"Depression is an epidemic," said Weber. "I don't know anyone who isn't. I'm not sure if it's the disconnect from nature, or because we are stripped from community-mindedness. We are not cougars, we are not solo creatures. We're wolves. We're pack animals." One reason for it being an epidemic could be that isolation helps make us susceptible to depression even as depression makes us seek isolation; it's the raising of that dark cone of power that secures depression in our lives.

One reaction that can feel very hurtful is toxic positivity, the idea that a positive mindset must be maintained, that no one wants to know about someone else's pain. Weber believes it's important to call that out. "There's a difference between focusing on the negative and acknowledging it," she said.

Ivo Dominguez, Jr. has a lot to say about the problems with that "everything happens for a reason" mindset, saying that it "comes with an expectation of a lesson, or grand plan, or larger forces that put [the obstacle] there for a reason. You can become subservient to finding what's meaningful, when your first duty may be to escape it." It's always possible to put together a full causal map with enough information, but "knowing why is not the same as something having an actual purpose. The idea is that things are purpose-driven. There are no clear, direct, simple answers, and seeking them can cause pain. If you assume it's purposeful, you're more likely to blame yourself or others. Humans can create purpose, but that's not the same as serving a purpose, or that it was ordained, which is where people sometimes get trapped. You are granting part of your will and magical power to supporting the circumstance."

I have fallen into this very trap. I am very set in my belief that my complaining can very well make things worse, learning from a young age that what one worried about usually came to pass. This is wrongheaded thinking; my parents were not worrying things into being, they were using their experience to avoid problems. While I am more than happy to listen to someone else's worries, I clam up when asked about mine. In time, I expect to drop that bad habit.

'Til Death Do Us Part

The idea that depression might be a lifelong companion can feel overwhelming or terrifying, but that's the negative spin one might expect when filtering the world through the lens of depression.

"The condition can be managed, but I'd be surprised if I were ever completely free of it," Sarah W. said. "In my twenties I would get bogged down for months at a time [and] could barely do anything spiritual" or work through basic life tasks, but "over time the intensity hasn't changed, but the duration has drastically. It's often much shorter, but while I'm in it [it feels] just as intense a state as it ever was. I can even sometimes dive to the bottom real quick. Fighting is not helpful to me, like how a Buddhist doesn't stop the thought [while meditating], just be aware and let it go. Fighting latches on, keeps it longer. I'll embrace it [and] allow myself a day or two go down the pit, feel it, and then, okay, that's it."

Now in my fifties, I have re-framed my relationship with depression: Rather than trying to avoid or prevent it, I seek to recognize it as quickly as possible. I too got bogged down terrifically in my 20s, and have seen the bouts become shorter in duration as I have aged. The brass ring I reach for is a reliable early-warning system. If I can avoid surpassing my stress threshold, I am less likely to experience depression. The tricky part is recognizing what adds stress in my life, and that's why I choose to cultivate mindfulness. This is a journey, and one that for me is much slower than I'd like. I expect that those who have more experience with meditation, being present, and other mindfulness exercises could reach the same point in much less time.

External factors easily feed into a cycle of depression, whether the condition was caused by them or not. It makes identifying a cause challenging, perhaps even unnecessary. I have thought long and hard about what "caused" my depression, but for me that desire to know gets turned back in on itself and feeds the self-recrimination and feelings of unworthiness that keep that ugly wheel tumbling along.

◄§ JOURNAL EXERCISE ❧
Rewriting Your Relationship with Depression

Set a timer for fifteen minutes.

Think of a recent day when you felt the weight of depression, and imagine that your world was entirely in black and white like it was in the beginning of the classic movie *The Wizard of Oz*. The lack of color reflects how you felt on that day. Now, write a story about that day in which you open the front door and the world is full of color again, and you can see and experience it free of depression once you step through that door. What's the first thing you'd do? What does the day feel like? Is the spirit of depression a character in your story at all, or do you write it out completely?

If your timer runs out while you're on a roll, it's okay to continue writing. You can also add to this story later on as a way to continue envisioning that life for yourself.

four
Depression and the Gods

Where are the gods?

One of the consequences of depression is a feeling of isolation, and that often extends to feeling cut off from the gods. I believe that even atheists suffer from this spiritual isolation; not knowing what you're missing doesn't mean that you're lacking it. The gods sustain us not necessarily by their actions or their attention, but by their presence. Their existence is not dependent upon belief, and their presence has beneficial effects even if we do not worship them, or even if we do not believe that they exist at all. Not being aware of the gods can feel crushing if one is used to being sensitive to their presence, but this should not be interpreted as rejection. This withdrawal is a natural part of relationships with deities and varies for reasons we will not always understand. When it occurs during depression, though, it can feel personal because in depression it's easier to jump to the worst conclusion—sometimes, even in the face of contrary evidence.

The typical depression mindset is as such: the gods have rejected me, or never cared about me in the first place, or do not actually exist. What's actually going on is that seeing the world through depression-colored glasses makes it easy to filter out or distort evidence of the gods. Were those three crows watching silently from a branch a sign, a rebuke, or completely overlooked because you've taken to looking at your feet when you're out walking instead of taking in the wonder of the world?

Depression derailed my religion for a time. When you're a member of a big church, people will notice when you skip services. If you practice on your own, no one asks about it. For those among us in that position—including me—it's easy to have religion derailed by depression. I wasn't sure how to honor the gods, and I wasn't sure if they cared. However, the gods exist whether or not we sense that they are near. Your depression cannot stymie the gods. There are times when they do not feel close, and depression can make that feel vindictive or personal, yet it is neither of these things. I eventually came to realize that the way to maintain a solitary religious practice is to do something every day.

One reason why a daily routine is important, no matter what one's path, is that spiritual muscle memory of practice. Use that regular time to ask for guidance out of this dark period. Since I'm a polytheist and I have relationships with several gods, once I recognize that depression is trying to slide inside again, I might add an offering to Demeter, who knows a thing or two about emotional loss and suffering, or Apollon, the healer who brings the light of truth to bear on the lies whispered by depression. Having those relationships already established makes a big difference. It's harder to begin a relationship than it is to maintain one under these conditions.

Where are the gods? They are where they were before, and where they will be after. It is not the gods who have changed, and being in depression does not make you any less worthy to give them honor or receive their blessings. It may make you less interested in the former, and less likely to notice the latter, and that's the cruel truth.

Gods come and go in our lives for reasons that are not always clear. Some of these cycles are related to the greater world, with seasons and conditions signaling when a particular deity may become more or less present. There are other reasons that are tied to the gods themselves, and about which we can only speculate. Our own mental states also seem to impact how present a god may be in our lives. Depression is certainly a mental state that impacts how we experience the divine. Some gods seem to withdraw, while others become more present. This change in relationships can itself cause distress, because when one is experiencing depression it's easy to assume that whatever is different is a form of punishment. The filters through which we perceive the world are bent in depression to make it easy to assume the worst.

Disconnection from natural cycles, such as through patriarchy and industrialization, have resulted in these wounds to our gods and their people by means of genocide direct and indirect. Paganism has a "special charge" in the face of this imbalance, which becomes evident in more ways almost with each passing day. By following those practices, Foxwood said, "We're the people of the roots of human civilization, and those roots got left behind... you cannot curse the roots and bless the fruits." Paganism often includes ancestral practices, and "taking on the wounds and sorrow necessary to have integrity in traditions like conjure, and others with strong ancestral currents, require us to do some redeeming in the great river of blood."

Framed this way it can seem daunting, but Foxwood brings it home by speaking of the folk wisdom of his mother: "All they need to do is farm and hunt," he recalled her saying, and get back in touch with the natural rhythms of life and death. This opens the door to normalizing grief and processing it in due course.

No matter the specific religious tradition that one practices, engaging in that religion can alleviate symptoms of depression. "I need my spiritual practices most when I am depressed, but that is when I am most likely to ignore them," said Weber, who has an early start time to the work day in order to coordinate with coworkers three time zones away, and "it's easy to roll out of bed and start working, but it's not a good way to live. Even just five minutes at the altar, lighting the candle, makes me a better person." She said she asks something to the effect of, "Let me be the best person I can be today, to take advantage of being awake and alive." On one occasion, "I went to my altar and cried for awhile. I'm not okay, but going to the altar helped me name it when my husband asked. It reminded me this is temporary and we will be okay on the other side of it. The gods won't cure it, but help me see what I need, the courage to say I feel like garbage and not okay, and to answer the question of what I need."

Depression can undermine spiritual practice, Foxwood agrees, and that can build upon itself. "When a person feels an obligation to a practice and its ideals...and we fall short, did we betray those ideals? If we miss daily practices, did we betray those gods and spirits, and does it cause depression to go deeper?" Falling short of oaths can compound that cycle.

Advice that Weber has been given is to "meditate every day for thirty minutes unless you're busy, then do it for an hour." She applies this to her religious practice: "You should go to your altar every day, but if you're in a bad place, go three times a day."

"If I am doing quiet time, and focusing on that regularly, it really does help pull me out of a really shitty mood for a few hours," Tenpenny said. "When it's really bad, it's hard to access that, but religion is a major solace in the depression," a source of emotional comfort. He mentions his partner's role with similar weight, saying that

Raven is also a source of structure and discipline, prompting him to do the things that keep him healthy. Others might find structure in a regular job, but Tenpenny lacks that outlet.

"Whatever has that tendency in me gets commingled with spiritual disconnection or emptiness," Sarah W. said. "I think other pagans and polytheists experience that, [and] they stop doing their devotions or magic. It's a terrible feedback loop [that] makes everything worse. Doing that work brings me back to myself, gets me out of that pit." To be clear, "the last thing I want to do is that work," and that's often what helps her realize she has slipped into that state, when doubts and negative self-talk "come to forefront" and "become more believable." Sarah W. rejects the condition by reiterating "that work," even when not feeling it at the time.

"I tend to go back to the basics in spirit work when I need to," Sarah W. continued. For her that means focusing "strongly to the devotional side, which for me is intertwined with magic and spirits," with "Dionysos primarily and uniquely suited to that problem." She even has a particular mantra for that god, which helps keep it simple. She recommends, "Say a prayer or even make the most basic offering, even if not feeling it, even when angry. Sometimes that does it. You don't have to feel it. [The] physical, tangible things in our practice mean you can do the external stuff; you may not hear the gods but they can hear you, and that has an impact even if you're not in the right mood for it."

Here's a list of deities who might have a particular interest in, or understanding of, depression. Keep in mind that all gods have their own personalities and preferences. If you are drawn to any of these deities, do some research to understand how best to make their acquaintance, and as Kaldera advises, "Make sure you divine on whether to ask someone before you propitiate them."

Apollo or **Apollon** is connected with both Greek and Roman pantheons. A god of healing, truth, and light, Apollo also has an interest in creative pursuits such as music and poetry that might be dampened during depression. In some traditions Apollo is said to drive the chariot of the sun across the sky, as well.

Consecrating a divination system to Apollo may make it easier to use during a period of depression.

Ares is a Greek god of battle, carnage, and war. The myths about this god are not entirely noble, but in one the god kills Hallirhothios, who raped Ares' child Alkippe, and was then acquitted by the other gods. Ares does not let anger fester, and instead acts. Ares is also difficult to ignore: during one battle, the god bellowed like nine thousand soldiers when wounded. During one particularly dark time when I felt isolated from the gods, Ares came to bellow at me like a holy drill sergeant, extolling me to stop being weak and instead to direct my anger at finding solutions. For me, those solutions included reorganizing my practice around Hellenic polytheism.

Offer your anger to Ares, especially if you do not know how to use it. Ares will help you hone and focus it, and thus release it rather than being consumed by it.

Blith is a Norse god of happiness and "head weather", as Kaldera explains: "In the shamanic healing system of [northern tradition shamanism], the body can be seen as a world unto itself, an ecosystem, and we are taught to journey inside someone's body, visualizing it as an entire world, and interpreting the ecosystem. In the apple valley, which is the brain, chemical imbalance sometimes shows up in these shamanic journeys as 'bad weather,' thus Blith, a minor Norse healing goddess whose name literally means 'happiness,' and who is called upon for healing mental illness and mood disorders by my tradition, is referred to as 'the goddess who calms the weather in the brain.'"

Ask Blith to calm the weather that rages in your own head. Try offering an apple to represent the apple valley, and ask the boon of a clear day of happiness.

Demeter is a Greek god of agriculture and the fertile earth. The abduction of Demeter's child Persephone forms the basis of myth explaining the existence of winter, and was the focus of one of the longest-running mystery cults in history. After that disappearance, Demeter lost hope and was inconsolable, resulting in the first winter.

Pray to Demeter for guidance on how to endure feelings of hopelessness, and ask for a sign that new life will again burst forth in your own heart.

Dionysos is a Greek god who is closely associated with mental health, madness, and liberation. "Instead of trying to get happy, it's about letting go of all that I feel," recounted Sarah W., a devotee of the god. Also closely associated with wine, Dionysos understands the subtle difference between using and abusing alcohol and other drugs. In one myth, Dionysos is torn limb from limb by enemies, only to be reborn in a more powerful form. The fact that depression is reminiscent of an underworld journey means that this rebirth is a hopeful sign that we can return from this difficult journey.

When life feels overwhelming and everything seems like it is spinning out of control, recite these words from Aelius Aristides: "nothing can be so firmly bound by illness, by wrath, or by fortune that cannot be released by Dionysos."

Frey or **Freyr** is a norse god of grain and agriculture, called the "golden one." As such, Frey is connected with the cycle of death feeding life that is systematized in agriculture. As with other gods on this list, Frey knows something of the mystery of death, but it seems that it's Frey's connection with light that makes this god a strong ally during periods of depression. Tenpenny shared an experience in which Frey placed a spark of light in Tenpenny's heart. "He told me this was light in the darkness, and I could build this into a fire to keep me warm in the dark times."

Call upon Frey to rekindle your own light and teach you to find your own way in the darkness.

Freya or **Freyja** is a Norse god of love and fertility, which in this case has an unambiguously sexual quality. Kaldera advises that while Freya may bless any sort of fertility, it's wise to set clear boundaries around pregnancy in any case. The body is the first place Freya will turn, and the body is often the repository for the accumulated emotions left to build up and stagnate during a period of depression.

Ask Freya to help you remember your love of life, and to use the gifts of your own body to feed your creativity, imagination, and passion.

Hekate is a Greek god who is described as "welcome in all the worlds": the living earth, starry heaven, and the underworld as well. It was Hekate who helped Demeter search the world for the missing Persephone, carrying a torch to light the way to the dark places. The dark of the moon, called *deipnon* in Hellenic practice, is a time when Hekate is asked to help clear out the old month to make way for the new.

Wiccans associate Hekate with the dark of the moon. In writing a book on Hekate, Weber found herself coming to terms with what it means to be the witch, who like that deity is "completely revered or evil and wicked, all of the above; she is a dangerous goddess. I walked through that process and understood that, and toward the end she said, 'This is who you are: the witch, the weird girl.'" Weber identified with being regarded in many different and powerful ways. "Like Hekate, people didn't like the way I look or talked, or idolized me as a savior. No, I'm just someone holding rituals. I'm not the perfect person."

Ask Hekate to light the way as you undertake shadow work and explore the darkness of depression. In the alternative, when the moon is dark, bring Hekate your doubts and fears and ask for them to be taken from you.

Hel or **Hela** is a Norse god of death, traditionally depicted with a body that is half alive and half expired. Hel is charged with caring for those who die of sickness and old age. Some devotees of Hela, such as Joshua Tenpenny, find themselves closer to this deity during periods of depression, when the god is experienced as a "loving, compassionate mother." Tenpenny reports that during such deep devotion, "the depression is irrelevant to that [relationship]. Maybe it's the key to access the experience."

Call upon Hel when you feel lost and near the point of breaking. In your prayer, make it clear that you do not know where to turn and that you seek solace.

Helios is the god who first directed the chariot of the sun across the sky each day, according to Greek mythology, and continues to be honored as a sun god by some devotees. This all-seeing god was the sole witness to the abduction of Persephone, for even the darkness of the underworld is thick enough to banish the light of day.

If you feel darkness encroaching, making it difficult for you to see the way forward or be willing to act, ask Helios to cast light upon your situation and allow you to see clearly.

Herne is a god of the hunt who is most strongly connected with Wicca. Herne is depicted as an antlered human man hunting to feed the people, and also as a stag who dies so that the people might eat. The cycle of predator and prey here serves as a reminder of how rare and precious life can be.

Call on Herne to remind you that others depend upon your skills and your presence in community, and that you are an important part of what makes your community thrive.

Himinglaeva is a Norse god, one of the nine daughters of Ægir and Rán who are described as mermaids or waves. Kaldera refers to Himinglaeva as the "ninth mermaid" and a bringer of light. The name has been taken to mean "transparent on top" in English, suggesting the light shining through a wave of emotion.

Pray that Himinglaeva will bring light when your emotions are roiled and you fear you may drown in your own feelings.

Inanna or **Ishtar** is a Mesopotamian deity with a great many associations. The most relevant myth here is of Inanna's descent into the underworld in an attempt to conquer it, which is a humbling experience that is characterized by giving up all that was precious to the god.

Ask Inanna for the resolve to see your journey through without ever forgetting who you are.

The **Morrigan** is a Celtic god of battle who models inner strength. Weber recalled that the process of writing *The Morrigan: Celtic Goddess of Magick and Might* was one of "coming to terms with places I'd failed myself," said Weber, when she had "given more away than I should through no one's fault but my own." While in the old myths the Morrigan is depicted mostly in the carnage of war, devotees who are experiencing an inner battle like one with depression also derive comfort from this god's strength.

Offer the Morrigan your pain and your suffering. This is an offering that may be readily accepted.

Persephone is a Greek god best known for being kidnapped, but who is also a god of flowers and springtime. Persephone was taken to the underworld to marry Hades, and ultimately adopted a routine of spending part of the year in the land of the dead and the remainder in that of the living. Persephone epitomizes the hope that even death is not forever, and that there is always some form of rebirth in the future. "When I was in the depths of bad depression and had no skills to manage it, I identified with Persephone in a metaphorical way," said Sarah W. "Her descent into darkness and return was important to me."

Ask Persephone for a sign that your own period of darkness will end, and because it's hard to see in the dark, ask too that the scales fall from your eyes so that you can see that sign in the first place.

Poseidon is the Greek god of the moving world, whether that's the storms and tides of the oceans or the world-wrenching power of earthquakes. This makes Poseidon a manifestation of the emotions that are buried so deeply that no one can predict when they will next erupt. The depths of the ocean are places of incredible darkness and unimaginable pressure. This same pressure that births devastating tsunamis can also bring forth new land.

Give Poseidon your grief and your sadness and ask that the salt of the ocean carry away your pain if you are unable to shed tears.

◄§ EXERCISE §►
Find Your Gods

The gods listed here are a very limited assortment, and the descriptions do not do any of them justice. The gods you should be turning to during depression may be in these pages, or entirely absent from them.

What you'll need:

- stories about gods, be they in books, on the internet, or from the lips of friends and co-religionists.

What you'll do:

1. Review the above list and see if any of the listed gods sparks some interest. If so, start digging into the stories from myth, and seek out any modern devotees you can find to see how the practice has evolved.

2. If this list is too limited, research the stories of gods your ancestors may have worshiped.

3. Continue your research, if needed, by asking other people online or in person about their experience with gods unfamiliar to you.

4. When you have found a deity that speaks to your spiritual condition, use divination to determine if the interest is mutual, and then meditate on how you should start your relationship. You may need to find a human teacher. A relationship with a god may be a long-term commitment; make sure you set clear boundaries at the outset and do not make any promises you are not entirely certain you can keep.

No matter the cosmology, it's common to see a cycle that feeds upon itself to grow stronger. This should be seen as not about blame, because it's no different than a feedback loop. The reaction is not *sub*conscious, I would say, but *un*conscious. There's no blame to assign. It would be easy to conclude, upon reading this, that it is hopeless and there is no way to stop this experience. This is also false. Depression can be managed, it can be treated, and it is possible to forget what it feels like to be depressed. The toll may be huge, but with help it can be borne, and there is always help to be had even if it's hard to recognize.

✎§ JOURNAL EXERCISE §❧
Thank-You Note

Set a timer for eight minutes.

Write a thank-you note to a god. You may name a god to whom you already pray or give offerings, or you may not know which god watches over you—in which case, you might ask to know that name.

Include a list of blessings in your life. You don't need solid proof that the god you're writing to made those good things happen; just list them and say thank you. Every person receives blessings, but it can be easy to overlook them during a period of depression. If this exercise is a struggle, set it aside for now and return to try again tomorrow. Your subconscious will help pick out the blessings you're receiving, and it will be much easier on the second try.

If you find that you cannot list all of your blessings before time runs out, return tomorrow and write another thank-you note because you are blessed indeed.

part two
Strategies for Life
with Depression

five
Strategies for the Body

The body and mind are both part of the same person, as much as the fingers and lungs are part of the same person. Just as damaging one part of the body can impact another—an ankle injury leading to back pain, for example—harm to any part of the body or mind can spread out to other aspects of the self, including the spiritual parts. Since Kari Tauring has declared "I think, therefore I am" dangerous because it has torn body and mind apart, let us for the moment focus on them together, as part of one whole. While I see depression as a spiritual condition first, it is often identified first through the body, or especially the mind.

Moving and Eating

Depression has a stagnation to it; it encourages us to slow down physically and mentally. Observing this, Kirk White pointed out that movement—*doing* something—can get both body and mind unstuck. The doing of something is a shift in the relationship. Perhaps most important is to "put one foot in front of the other" and continue to make steps on the path of life, no matter how difficult. "Breathing is most important when you have asthma," White said to illustrate the point, despite how hard it can be to do it. "The first full breath back is ecstatic." Choosing not to breathe is choosing to die, and that's not something most people will give in to without a fight. Giving in to the stagnation of depression—choosing to do nothing—is just as dangerous, although it can take months or years to succumb to death from depression alone.

During a period of depression, a counselor convinced White to sign a contract just to take a walk daily, invoking the power of one's own word to make a change. Creating a contract like this is a way to hold oneself accountable, by making the commitment an external one. It uses the same motivational power we usually reserve for other living beings in our lives, such as pets. "People without kids and animals to care for have the luxury of being depressed," White said. He and his wife reared one child to adulthood, and maintain a constant stream of animals at their Laurelin Retreat Center that have included dogs, cats, llamas, pygmy donkeys, and chickens. "You just have to get out of bed" when there are life-and-death issues to consider, because "somebody needs me." I would have thought the opposite was true, but I had no external responsibilities during my worst period of depression: I'd dropped out of college, my pet was living with my parents, and my landlords were too kind to press me on the fact that I'd bartered work on the apartment for a place to live. Upon reflection, I see how having pets and a stepchild and a spouse and a mortgage have all helped me push through periods of depression that I've experienced since.

It's important to celebrate any movement made, too, and I mean *any* movement, even if it's something as simple as getting up and dressed in clean clothes. Inertia is a powerful force whether it's reinforcing motion or stillness, and just because the first push against it doesn't appear to yield much doesn't mean it didn't take a huge amount of effort. Just as Atlas would not have the strength to lift a pencil on top of bearing the weight of the heavens, someone with depression is expending most strength just on existing. Even minor accomplishments, therefore, are bigger than they seem. Acknowledge the effort and never, ever downplay it.

The value of this cannot be emphasized enough. Any action, no matter how small, is a victory—even if it feels woefully insignificant. Continents are not shifted across the face of the globe in one day; they are moved imperceptibly and it takes an incredible amount of force to make that happen. When you accomplish one small thing—taking a shower, opening the mail, walking around the block—you are channeling as much energy as some people would to run a marathon, and that should be acknowledged. As a priest of Poseidon, I have learned to invoke him as Ennosigaios—earth-shaker—to help make those small things happen when the inertia set against me feels vast.

There is some evidence that depression is linked to inflammation, and that like inflammation it has served an evolutionary purpose in healing and minimizing the spread of infection and disease. If that is the case, then taking steps to reduce inflammation might also reduce the effects of depression. These include:

- exercise,
- probiotics
- diet

This last one makes a big difference: high levels of sugar and refined carbohydrates (sorry, fellow bread-lovers) including sweet desserts, processed meats and junk foods, soybean and corn oils, trans-fats, and alcohol can all increase inflammation in the body. Instead, try to eat foods that come from a recognizable source like fruits, vegetables, and tree nuts; olive and coconut oil, fatty fish like salmon and sardines, dark chocolate, green tea, and even small amounts of red wine.[30]

᥍ EXERCISE ᥏
Make a Shopping List

What you'll need:

• writing implement and writing surface.

What you'll do:

Bad nutrition feeds depression, and poor planning can lead to bad nutrition. We eat what's around when we are hungry, and we can take control of what's around with a shopping list. Since even the simplest task can seem overwhelming during depression, it may help to begin by reciting this prayer to do one small thing:

> *Shining ones, if you will it,*
> *may I see past the fog*
> *to do this small thing.*

Pick up the pen and write down whatever foods come to mind. Either jot down ingredients you've cooked with before, or meals that someone in your household might prepare if asked—including you. Visualize what you imagine eating at home, and go from there. Don't be concerned about whether it's good for you—frozen dinners are a step in the right direction if you get all your meals in a drive-through lane. Commit to preparing some of the food yourself, even if it's only rarely. You can improve the quality and the quantity of the meals made at home as you do this exercise again.

---

30. "Anti-Inflammatory Diet 101," Healthline, accessed April 18, 2021, https://www.healthline.com/nutrition/6-foods-that-cause-inflammation.

If you're stuck on coming up with even one recipe, think about the meals you've enjoyed with other people. What did you eat? Who prepared it? Ask that person for the recipe and try it out. If it doesn't taste like you remembered it, you can go back to that person and ask for advice. Everyone wants to feel needed, and it's easier to talk about cooking than it is depression.

Depression is a condition that impacts body, mind, and spirit, and addressing it through the needs of the body should not be ignored. "Encourage your depressed clients to eat a healthy low-chemical diet, to get enough sleep (but to make themselves get up if they are sleeping too much), to exercise even if only gently, to get out in the sun, to get out in nature, to sing if they have that interest, to get massage or other nice physical sensations, and to garden if they're into it—getting one's hands in the dirt has an antidepressant effect," explained Raven Kaldera. "Emphasize that these activities are not curative, but can help one survive the storm. However, nothing helps if you don't do it. Encourage them to take a buddy if necessary."

Movement and exercise, even in small amounts, can begin to break down the pattern of behavior that reinforces depression. At its most extreme, depression can leave a body sitting on the couch or lying in a bed for most or all of the day, and even getting up and staying up and walking around the room is an improvement. Exercise for its own sake is not an easy habit to form, and it requires discipline that may be absent during a period of depression. Any action can be beneficial for breaking up the inertia of depression, but it might be easier to start with something physical. Small steps are fine, because they are motion; what you're trying to avoid is stagnation, falling into a pattern that does not lead to any change in your circumstances, your behavior, or how you feel. Exactly what physical action to add depends on the present situation.

Are you spending a lot of waking hours in bed? Next time you get up for any reason, delay returning. Add a trip to the kitchen or bathroom, or empty the trash. You might even swing past a household altar, taking some time to straighten or dust some of the icons.

Has the couch become a sinkhole? If that's the case, the remote control is not your friend. It's just too easy to watch hour after hour of programming or videos on one screen or another. When the next bit of content is about to start, hit "pause" and take a stretch break. If you planned on setting up a snack, why not pop your head outside for a few minutes first? Just a simple amble around the perimeter of the building or yard can be enough to start. When you get back, take a moment to turn off the auto-play feature on the television, and then find a new place to keep that remote control: it should be within sight, but out of reach, so you have to get up to use it.

Taking on a hobby might bring with it a certain amount of joy or fascination that allows for concentration to be held. Hobbies tend to engage both body and mind, with the amount of movement and concentration varying depending on the one selected. They can also encourage the social interaction that is quite beneficial for mitigating symptoms of depression.[31]

Tenpenny understands that some people do physical ordeals as part of this work, but "it's not my thing at all. It's unpleasant and doesn't do it for me. I got the endorphins, but it didn't go anywhere, like [cocaine]. Ultra-marathons as a spiritual experience, in the mountains for days with no food? Nope, not me." However, these

---

31. Daisy Fancourt, et al., "Fixed-Effects Analyses of Time-Varying Associations between Hobbies and Depression in a Longitudinal Cohort Study: Support for Social Prescribing?" *Psychotherapy and Psychosomatics* (2019). DOI: 10.1159/000503571

things do work for other people, and he believes in trying new tools and techniques. "I've tried a lot of stuff," he said.

Using the massive endorphin surge that comes from intense exercise is an effective way to manage depression, and I salute anyone who does become a triathlete, or builds log cabins by hand, or embraces other intense physical experience on a regular basis. Not everyone is going to dive into that, in part because getting motivated to make big changes is not easy during depression, but also because—as Tenpenny notes—for many people, it feels like trading one unpleasant experience for different one. It reminds me how housekeeping is a form of devotion to Hestia, but visitors to my home would never guess by tidiness alone that I have a relationship with that god. If you have the passion and capacity to jump into physical activity this completely, feel free! I cannot offer you advice on doing it safely and successfully, but rest assured your interest shows that you're already well on your way to breaking depression's hold.

The importance of healthy sleep should not be overlooked. "For some people who have chronic suicidal ideation, it may be a sign that they need some simple self-care, like a nap," Rella told me. If a nap can save a life, that's good to remember. Sleep patterns can become disrupted during depression, and then we further blur the lines if we choose to remain in bed, or in our sleep clothes, for much of the day. The first step toward a regular sleep routine is to set a bedtime and stick with it. Half an hour before bedtime, disconnect from screens. The light from many of them can disrupt falling asleep, as can the way the mind races from news story to cat video and back. Take that thirty minutes to allow the mind to slow down. Drink a cup of herbal tea, leaf through a magazine or a favorite book, talk to a family member, but don't use technology. The world can wait. The next step to regularize sleep is to get out of bed, get washed up, and get dressed once you're awake. Master that, and it will become a bit easier to stick to that regular bedtime.

Thinking and Feeling

Having separate words for body and mind reinforces what Kari Tauring says is the most dangerous idea in the western world, that our bodies and minds are separate, not part of the same person. That this is false can be seen in the impact of bodily actions on emotions. Gritting teeth and clenching fists until one is trembling feels very much like trembling with rage, and breathing quickly and shallowly can generate anxiety or fear. This is because while thoughts come from the mind, the emotions that color them stem from the body. Something of a feedback loop can be created, for example, with anger coloring thoughts that return to the mind thus angered, begetting more angry actions that put the body in a state to generate more anger. The same can happen with self-deprecating thoughts, creating that internal voice that consistently cuts oneself down. Tending to the needs of both body and mind are essential for managing a period of depression because the vulnerability that allows it entry could be in either.

Siobhan Johnson has found success in discarding the arbitrary distinction between "health" and "mental health," and instead assuming that basic care for illness remains the same. "I find it helps to treat this like I would a physical ailment and to ask the people around me to do the same. There's a lot of mileage in rest, good food, and the other things you'd do if it was a cold, or the flu, or something like that. Stay hydrated."

Since emotions are housed in the body—something that is clear to anyone who has become grumpy on an empty belly—they can sometimes be released directly through the body. "Muscle massage, even without deliberate acupressure, can produce surprising results for relief of anxiety and depression. Some massage therapists have witnessed the sudden release of emotion that comes with activation of a trauma memory. Muscle memory trauma release can happen unexpectedly in the course of massage therapy for depression, pain, or injury … it is an unexpected bonus for healing the mind."[32] In one study of massage, 75 percent of participants had a reduction in depression, a result comparable to what is found for therapy.[33] Another healing modality that begins with the body is acupuncture. With those hair-thin needles placed at the correct points, acupuncture can promote healing of the mind by affecting the limbic system.[34]

Putting the body in motion can also put the emotions in motion. The body is where they live, and moving our limbs is one of the ways we can process them. This doesn't have to mean long hours of training to compete in a triathlon, but it should involve moving more today than you did yesterday. If it helps, set reminders that it's time to move and use a timer. Even if you're only moving for thirty seconds, if it's more than you were moving then it's a positive change. Make a commitment to extend the amount of time at least once a week to make sure that you continue to move more and more.

Depression is characterized by slowing down and stagnation, even though the thoughts we experience can feel like they are coming very fast. In my experience, it's not that there are too many thoughts to process so much as there are a few thoughts that are being repeated endlessly. Another way to look at it is as if your mind is generating thoughts at normal speed, but your ability to process those thoughts and all the emotions associated with them is slowed down—depressed. This slowing down is not entirely on the inside,

---

32. Wanck, *Mind Easing*, 162.

33. Wanck, *Mind Easing*, 165.

34. Wanck, *Mind Easing*, 166–7.

either; other people sometimes will notice that someone experiencing depression is slower to act or react. It feels exhausting, and is expressed as brain fog and mental paralysis.

You have the power to contribute to your own healing. This is not an accusation, it is an affirmation. Yes, it is true that there are times when someone is in such a deep crisis that this idea is beyond them, and those people especially might benefit from professional help that could include prescription medication. The spark of healing can be weakened or extinguished if it is not tended, and medication is one way to rekindle it. For most of us, at most times during our lives, that spark still burns brightly in the darkness. The terrible, paradoxical truth is that we can become convinced of our own helplessness far more often than we can actually be rendered helpless. It does not serve depression for its companion human to pray, or seek out positive people, or exercise, or care for a pet, or to work magic, or to accept help from a mental health professional. We do not need studies to identify what thoughts and activities weaken the hold depression has on a person; all we need do is see what someone experiencing depression avoids! Invariably, we avoid the behaviors that weaken the grip, such as eating wholesome food, or meditating, or accepting invitations to spend time with other people.

"When you've exceeded your stress threshold and you feel anxious or depressed, you'll need to reduce your stress," writes psychiatrist Bick Wanck. "Ways to reduce stress include saying no to unnecessary activities [and] remembering to breathe."[35] What Wanck doesn't discuss is how one ends up near that stress threshold in the first place. Here's one possibility: "If I say no to this request, this person may never speak to me again." That fear leads us to bite off more than we can chew. We surpass that personal stress threshold, and

---

35. Wanck, *Mind Easing*, 38.

suddenly we can't handle any of these obligations. We feel like a failure and withdraw from anyone who reminds us of that emotion. It's a negative feedback loop of emotion, what I think of as depression's dark cone of power, and once someone is caught in it they might find themselves exceeding that stress threshold again and again, getting buffeted each and every time.

Aging

My own experience affirms the anecdotes that I have collected: it gets easier to manage depression as one gets older, if only because it becomes easier to recognize it more quickly and start addressing it before it becomes overwhelming. I cannot promise it will ever be a walk in the park, though. Even as I was writing this book I had a wave of depression so strong come over me that I had to cut off several ongoing obligations just to get this project done, including my only paying job. I knew my spoons were dropping fast and that I would do more damage to myself and others if I didn't act quickly, because even with some experience it still seemed to catch me unawares. Cutting down on my obligations was the best way to preserve my community ties in the long run, but I did beat myself up a bit for putting myself in a position where it was necessary. There are just times when I require a simplification of my life to avoid, or manage, a period of depression. Since these cycles happen over years, it is not a quick process to learn the patterns and the signs.

Emerging from a period of depression means being willing and able to engage fully with the world again. It's living in sunlight; but just as darkness is not eternal, sunlight does not last forever. In times of darkness, we naturally seek to rest and withdraw, lay in firewood, and stock the shelves with canned goods. Emotionally it is the same, and what sometimes happens for me is that I commit myself to a reasonable amount of work, recreation, and service without considering whether I can maintain the same energy during a period of depression, should one arise. As with anything worth mastering, it takes patience and mindfulness to recognize those little triggers that jingle softly and bring depression around for a visit. Becoming an expert on one's depression journey is something that comes from necessity, not curiosity. My patience and self-awareness come entirely from this need. Depression is a difficult teacher, but I have grown much from the lessons.

six
Strategies for the Mind

Depression speaks to the nonverbal part of ourselves, whether we refer to this as the subconscious, the younger self, the id, or by some other term. Depression drains out the hope and the optimism along with the energy, making it easier to drop the ball and harder to recover emotionally from social gaffes and recriminating self-talk. We reinforce expectations of the worst case, fulfilling our own prophecies. "'Fake it 'til you make it' has effectiveness," Sarah W. believes. "It's not blase, it's communicating to your subconscious. Your emotions will catch up if you act the way you want to be acting." In effect, we are asking our conscious mind to lead by example if we "fake it," to go through the motions of an ideal day to train that part of the soul to expect that things are changing.

Approaches to managing depression can include anything with personal resonance, says Sarah W. Breathing techniques are a go-to for regulating mood, but she also suggests purification using a familiar practice rather than trying something new, if possible. Trusting what's familiar is worthwhile, because while the spiritual aspect will work regardless of one's mindset, "the psychological tends to be personal."

Shame is one of the ways that depression preserves itself. The emotion is one we recoil from or avoid, the same way that someone with a bad knee recoils from or avoids putting too much weight on that leg. Pain is a warning that something is wrong, and just avoiding the tender part isn't necessarily going to heal it. "To stop judging yourself and start seeing yourself as you are, you'll need to develop your curiosity. If you are curious about what you feel, what you think, and how you behave, you are more likely to view yourself objectively and less likely to judge yourself unkindly."[36] Since it's being used as a defense mechanism, the sense of shame may even increase under the scrutiny of curiosity, but anyone who is strong enough to live under the thumb of depression is more than up to the task of enduring a short-term backlash. I find that on difficult days it helps me to remind myself that even though the source of my challenges seems untiring, I remain in control of how I see the world. It is my curiosity about the source of my feelings that proves that this is true, because the only illegitimate feeling is one that comes from an external source, like depression. The emotional response in the form of shame is supposed to push me away, and that means I'm on the right track.

Tracking Mood

The reason why it's valuable to track one's mood is because human memory is not like a computer's. Our brains do not record events in a way that most of us can replay as we might a video recorder. Rather, when we key into a particular moment, we reconstruct what happened based on past history and context, among other cues.[37] It's similar to how we process visual information, which also relies

---

36. Wanck, *Mind Easing*, 47.

37. Vedantam, Shankar, host. *Hidden Brain: a conversation about life's unseen patterns.* "Did That Really Happen? How Our Memories Betray Us." Aired December 16, 2019 on NPR. https://www.npr.org/2019/12/16/788422090/did-that-really-happen-how-our-memories-betray-us.

heavily on filling in gaps based on existing patterns. That works well enough most of the time, but during periods of depression, we are already predisposed to emphasizing the negative over the positive. The result is that we tend to forget moments of happiness and joy, because they don't fit the narrative of constant misery.

Mood trackers can be as simple as a memo pad or as robust as a full-featured mood journal app for a smartphone. All one needs to do is jot down the first emotion that comes to mind, along with the date and time. A mood tracker can disprove notions of not having any emotions, or that you only experience the negative ones; over time, it can also show patterns of mood that can be broken by changing up routine. Tracking several times a day is more helpful than just once, because moods change over time. This tool is only effective if it's used, which is why I recommend setting several daily reminders just to log those emotions. I picked a time in the mid-morning, one in the early afternoon, and a third sometime in the evening. I also try to log my mood first thing when I wake up, and just before retiring for the night. Each reminder might only take moments to get the mood recorded.

Tracking mood is also an opportunity to do an emotional self-check. Depression can sneak up on a person, Sarah W. has found, even after a lifetime of living with the condition. She has learned to recognize the signs in herself. "When I stop listening to music," is one. "It's important to me ... I connect to emotional and spiritual stuff through it. That's not good, when it doesn't feel like it means anything." Some mood log apps include spots to record other information, like diet and medications, activities, weather, and more. Identify patterns and it may be possible to name depression more quickly.

Keeping a Journal

Tracking mood alone is keeping a very simple form of journal, but once you're in that habit, you can expand it; this is an opportunity to process some of those emotions using a keyboard or pen.

◀§ EXERCISE §▶
Protecting a Journal

In order for a journal to be a useful tool, you need to trust that whatever you write won't be used against you. Otherwise, you may hold back and miss out on the potential for healing and growth that should be available. Whether you write entries on paper, save them in a file on a computer, or post them to a blog, these words are intended to be private and it's okay to protect them. Here are some suggestions:

1. Silence: If no one knows that you keep a journal, no one is going to look for it. Keeping silent about the existence of your journal is a simple form of protection, but it's only easy if you can keep a secret.

2. Letters: If you know a different form of writing, use it. This could be a language like Tagalog, different letters like the Theban script, a technical system like the international phonetic alphabet, or an ancient writing system such as ogham that's been transliterated into the English alphabet. I remember meeting a senior citizen once who took notes in shorthand years after retirement, not because it's faster, but because no one else could decipher them. If it's something you will not forget how to read, consider using it. This may be only a thin layer of protection, if the people who share your home also share your background or interests.

3. Safekeeping: You can store your journal in a file cabinet, lock-box, or safe for which only you have the key. Add symbols of invisibility or protection inside the container to give the lock a boost. If your journal is electronic, learn how to make strong passwords and look into using a password manager app so you don't have to memorize it.

4. Warning: You can make it plain that reading your journal has consequences. "You who hold this book, beware: if you did not write the words within, then you bring harm to the writer and our relationship by reading any further. If you violate this sacred trust, what comes next will be entirely your responsibility." I put this inside the cover because I try to keep silent about my journal.

5. Misdirection: Don't put your moods or intimate thoughts in a leather-bound tome with the word "journal" embossed on the cover. Instead, make it look like something much less interesting, like an algebra notebook or business travel deductions. What's boring does not generate curiosity.

6. Honesty: Tell the people who might come across this book that it is your journal, and that you use it to process emotions. It's not secret, but it is private, because you are not ready to share these thoughts with other people yet. This is a good move if you're unlikely to be able to keep your journal a secret or hidden from them. Ask them to respect your healing process.

7. Spellfire: An alternative approach used by one of my early teachers was to write out a spell on the inside cover, one that called upon the universe—for the good

of all and according to the free will of all—to protect this book by taking all the harm that might befall you if someone were to read the book, and have it befall the reader instead. The next step, I recall my teacher explaining, was to "tell everyone about the spell."

Medication

I've touched upon prescription medication within "Your Relationship with Depression," in part one of this book, but it's worth rehashing just a bit. Psych medications alter brain chemistry. They are powerful tools, which may open up doors to healing never imagined possible. These drugs also have a variety of potential side effects, including changes to psychic perception. The right "med for your head" is life-changing, because it will allow the patient to get to a point where healing is finally possible. Unfortunately, medicine isn't advanced enough for doctors to be able to guarantee that the first one tried is going to do the trick. If it's been suggested to you that a doctor-supervised medication should be part of your treatment plan for depression, take that advice seriously. Ask about potential side effects of the drug you're being asked to take. Understand how long it will take to know if it's helping, and commit to tracking your moods to keep a more objective measure of any changes. If you agree to take a prescription drug for depression, don't alter the dose or stop taking it without talking to your doctor first—changing a drug like this is a time when the patient should be under close supervision.

"Medication is a tricky subject," said Raven Kaldera. "I never tell a client to go off their meds in favor of my [shamanic] ceremonies. If dissatisfaction with their provider comes up in the reading or the counseling session, I might encourage them to find someone they like better. If they are having trouble with their meds,

I encourage them to talk to their provider, and perhaps find a more responsive one. If it comes up in a reading that medication would do them good, I start by asking them how they feel about it, rather than giving it as advice. If they are resistant, I might ask, 'What would you do if you learned that this definitely had a strong chemical component? I'm not saying I'm sure that's so, I'm just asking what you'd do,' and go from there."

Joshua Tenpenny was first given a prescription at the age of fifteen, but the doctor didn't warn that it could have sexual side effects—because it was assumed a teenager wouldn't be sexually active. After some failed attempts, Tenpenny was prescribed a medicine that has worked well, and has become an important part of how the condition is managed. "I get lots of advice, but without the meds none of it worked. On meds, I try and they work. I need to do the things, I can do the things, and they help."

Medication is intended to treat the brain and body, but side effects can bleed over into the non-physical aspects of self. "The shamans in our tradition, as well as spirit-workers in other traditions, have exchanged a fair amount of hard-won information about what psychiatric medications do to innate psychic gifts," said Kaldera. "The general consensus, after some personal experiences and some observed ones, is that while some meds may cut down on psychic sensitivity at first for some people, if it's a good med for your head, psychic gifts will slowly return over a period of half a year or so. This means that if you've been on a med for more than a year and your gifts are still blocked, your body is not happy with that med, and you should look into that for many reasons, but telling a newly-medicated client that the potential blockage is normal, and might just pass with time, can be very helpful."

In addition to side effects, not every drug is going to be useful in the long run. "In my work as a mental health therapist, I've noticed that sometimes people experience very encouraging initial results with medications, only to have those taper off and become more moderate as the body adjusts," Anthony Rella said. "This is particularly painful for those who see a glimpse of a life that the sufferer couldn't have imagined before, and allow themselves to hope, only to feel crushed when things even out." Adjusting to a new medication is a time when it might be particularly useful to track one's moods throughout the day, so that these data can be shared with a therapist or psychiatrist. Memory of one's own moods is not to be trusted, and writing it down in the moment yields a more useful record.

Prescription drugs can mean the difference between life and death—or between life and a shadow of life—if the medicine is a good fit. Not everyone is going to be comfortable taking a pill, and not everyone who does will find the best match on the first try because there's a lot we still do not know about how these pills even work. This is an important decision, one that should be made with as much information as possible, and ideally while consulting with family members or trusted loved ones.

Ꮖ JOURNAL EXERCISE Ꮗ
Flash Moods

You'll need to set a series of reminders for this exercise. If you have a phone or other personal device that supports multiple alarms, then before bed set thirteen reminders for tomorrow. Space them out during the time you should be awake, and schedule them for oddball times like 10:54 and 3:27. If you only have a simpler system like a basic alarm clock or a kitchen timer, each time it goes off restart it to sound again in 36 minutes, until you've reached 13 times total; increase or decrease that 36 minutes to make sure you'll be awake each time it goes off.

Keep your journal within reach for the entire day. When the alert sounds, name the first emotion that comes to mind and write it down, along with the time. Do not second-guess your answer: write down the very first emotion that comes into your mind, and close your journal.

This will give you a clearer picture of how you felt throughout the day.

seven
Strategies for Spirit

Depression's voice encourages us to behave in ways to fulfill its own needs, but often not very helpful for the individual who is living with it. A spirit itself, it can leave our own spirit feeling bruised and beaten. It's possible that this spirit doesn't mean harm at all, but that doesn't make it hurt less. Helping one's own spirit to heal involves exploring the nature of the harm, finding allies, and reintegrating the whole self.

The idea that the purpose of depression is to aid the tribe by encouraging a sick individual to avoid other people is an intriguing possibility, although it's not one that has been proven yet. Certainly people experiencing depression tend to withdraw and become more isolated, not feeling like very good company and not wanting to have company either. Even if depression once was a condition that saved lives, so was sickle cell anemia, which swaps out a shortened, painful life for the near-certain quick death of malaria. Any evolutionary benefits of depression have long been supplanted by modern medicine, but this is a tenacious spirit with a job to do, even if nobody asked. It whispers suggestions that are hard to ignore since they are coming from inside our own heads. But by recognizing that this is a voice of a different person than yourself, it's possible to question this advice as you might from any other person.

The goal of depression appears not just to isolate us from other humans, but from other spirits, as well. Practices such as making offerings, celebrating holy days, remembering ancestors, and attuning our many aspects of self to one another often fall away during a period of depression. Just as it can require tremendous effort to accomplish small tasks while experiencing depression, the first steps toward changing this relationship might feel pointless. They are not. You are a spirit having a physical experience, meaning that you have power you have yet to fully tap. Reading through this section might trigger a twinge deep inside, a response of that spirit to the work. Lean into that twinge. Recognize what approaches resonate, because that spirit knows what it needs for healing, as does the body.

In its simplest form, the advice to manage depression is to do the opposite of what depression asks. "It's doing the spirit work that gets me out of that state, every time," that gets Sarah W. out of that rut. That's a theme that comes up again and again. Courtney Weber finds that spending more time at the altar is key, while Joshua Tenpenny visits a pool that is sacred to Frey.

Our tendency to avoid these activities feels like instinct, but as Orion Foxwod asked, "When a person feels an obligation to a practice and its ideals ... and we fall short, did we betray those ideals? If we miss daily practices, did we betray those gods and spirits, and does it cause depression to go deeper?" It is understandable to question why you should turn to your gods and spirits, but give yourself the gift of including another human person in that conversation as a sounding board. As difficult as that can sometimes feel, humans anchor one another in the world in a way that no one else can.

Meditation

I think of meditation as grounding and centering for the sake of grounding and centering. Pagans often talk about "grounding and centering" as if this is one action, but they are not. "Becoming grounded is about getting rid of excessive energy in the body, allowing clean energy to come through," according to psychologist Diana Raab, while, "Becoming centered is a way to find peace within the chaos that might be surrounding us."[38] Grounding keeps us from bouncing off the walls, and centering is about remembering who we are once we are still. Meditation is a way to accomplish both and, like everything that can be helpful during a period of depression, it's something that no one in depression is keen on trying.

An unusual grounding technique that is written about in *How to Heal Yourself When No One Else Can* by Amy Scher calls for a stainless steel spoon.[39] The spoon is used to trace intersecting lines over the tops of one's feet to break up energy blockages and get things moving. That's just the kind we use in our kitchen, but as this one was going to be applied to the feet I thought it best to conscript a spoon not already destined to spend time in my mouth. Obtaining a single spoon is not that easy; they tend to travel in packs of eight or a dozen. There are plenty of antique stores where spoons are sold, but they're all sterling or silver plate. One afternoon I drove past a thrift store and realized that this is where I could find flatware sold individually. I was correct, but I wasn't prepared. I had no cash on hand, and while the cashier wouldn't say there was a minimum, it was obvious she didn't want to run a card for

---

38. Raab, Diana. "What Is Centering? What Is Grounding?" Psychology Today, February 3, 2020. https://www.psychologytoday.com/us/blog/the-empowerment-diary/202002/what-is-centering-what-is-grounding.

39. Amy Scher, *How to Heal Yourself When No One Else Can*, (Woodbury, MN: Llewellyn Publications, 2016) 62.

ninety-nine cents plus tax. I offered to run home for the dollar—
I was only a few blocks away—but a man filling out a job application said, "I'll pay for that spoon for you." His kindness made me
smile, but as I was leaving I thought about how else I could have
taken his offer: did he think I couldn't afford a spoon, darn him? A
scene in which I took umbrage unfolded before me, and I smiled
again at my good fortune. I felt blessed, and because I chose to see
his act as a blessing, I *was* blessed. My agathos daimon—the spirit
which in Hellenic tradition brings fortune to one's life—whispered
in my ear, and I heard the message. What more blessing than that
do I ever need?

When I have tried this method of spoon grounding, I combined
it with something else Scher recommends: reciting an affirmation. I
use "I am well, I am whole" while I'm breaking up those blockages.

According to Barbara Rachel, "Meditation is, at its most basic,
sitting and paying attention without grasping, or focusing on a
mantra or phrase. Depending on who the person is, one of these
should work at some level." However, that's going to require some
patience. "It is first important to release expectations of what it
can do for you. Meditation is not the short road to enlightenment,
it is the gradual journey of quieting the mind. Since a depressed
person is often immobile, I recommend that they might as well
remain that way and just watch their thoughts as they come and
go like clouds in the sky, like the river slipping by, or a train passing.
It doesn't matter if you are sitting or lying down or walking down
the road, you can turn your attention to your thoughts, and in that
way gain some distance from them and from your depression. It
can be helpful just to watch, and return to noticing the breath over
and over when thoughts get crazy."

Emptying the mind can seem confusing, which is why returning
to noticing the breath is helpful because by focusing the attention

on something neutral, it helps limit the number of thoughts. There are other ways to create focus: gaze into a candle flame, a bowl of water, or passing clouds; burn the same kind of incense during a meditation session; recite a mantra silently or aloud; or play a track of meditation music or shamanic drumming. If there is one particular memory, thought, or feeling that you are struggling to release in meditation, consider a different tack: lean in. Use this particular thought as the focus, and allow it to unfold as you observe it dispassionately. Sitting with a specific thought and its role in your life is a form of shadow work, which is explored in more depth in the section by that name.

Not everyone can sit or lie still, and for those people Rachel suggests looking into yoga, calling it "meditation in motion—a way to stay present through doing something. Movement can break obsessive thoughts. In Alcoholics Anonymous they say, 'move a muscle, change a thought,' so if repetitive thoughts are an issue, people can consider just standing up and getting a glass of water to break the spell. The act of noticing without judgement helps us realize that we are not our depression, or our thoughts, or our situation. We are more timeless than that. We can discover the witness that is our true self."

If you are unsure if you can meditate at all, try this exercise.

◆§ EXERCISE §◆
Micro-Meditation

What you'll do:

Find a place that is free of distractions, and you can sit or lie down undisturbed. Lie flat or sit with your back straight and set a timer for one minute. Close your eyes and allow your thoughts to rise. Acknowledge each thought as it is created, but then give yourself permission to release it. When the timer goes off, open your eyes.

You may find that a surprising number of thoughts can run through your head in just one minute. I find that the first minutes of meditation are the most infuriating for me, because the brain requires time to slow down. This may be why so many people believe that they can't meditate at all. The goal with micro-meditation is simply to get into the routine of sitting with oneself at all. Then, we can deepen the practice.

You can build on your success with incremental meditation.

◆§ EXERCISE §◆
Incremental Meditation

What you'll do:

Return to your preferred place to be alone with your thoughts and not be disturbed. Sit with your back upright, or lie down flat, as you prefer. Set your timer for one minute longer than you set it the last time you meditated. Close your eyes, allow your thoughts to rise, and remember to release each one in turn. When the timer goes off, open your eyes.

What I have discovered is that each additional minute I sit in meditation is a minute with fewer thoughts to acknowledge. The mental clutter at the beginning can be so full that I actually get rapid-eye movements, even though I'm awake! My eyes tend to relax during the first minute, though, and are no longer distracting. By the third minute, I sometimes forget that I'm meditating, even while I'm doing it. The goal of incremental meditation is to increase the length of time to twenty minutes, although you could choose to go even longer if you prefer. If you don't wish to get there in just twenty sessions, that's fine too—add an extra minute every other session, or every fifth or tenth, whatever pace works for you.

Guided Meditation

Another way that a session can be given focus is as a guided meditation, in which you mentally follow a script that you have reviewed thoroughly ahead of time, or arrange for it to be read aloud. Guided meditation is intended to help you have a specific experience, as in the following examples, but I have found that sometimes my experience takes a 90-degree turn from reality and I end up meeting gods or discovering hidden knowledge that has nothing to do with the script. That's because sometimes I need a distraction from the here and now to open myself to deeper experience, and the guided meditation provides that opportunity. For the most part, a guided meditation is a way to relax into a narrative as a way to free yourself from other thought.

◄§ EXERCISE §►
Guided Meditation: To Receive the Gift of Stars

What you'll do:

Settle into a comfortable position and begin meditating. Arrange with a friend to begin reading the following, or record yourself reading it ahead of time to play now. In the alternative, study the following paragraph with care, and allow it to unfold before your mind's eye as you meditate. Keep your physical eyes closed.

As time passes in silence, you are becoming more and more aware of the surroundings beyond your closed eyelids. Echoing sound reveals walls, trees, and other objects; smells bring to mind nearby objects and beings. Without opening your eyes, you are able to clearly picture all the details that would be within sight. You look up, and as you do there is a change: a shimmer passes before you, and the starry night sky extends from horizon to horizon. The view is so clear that you feel you could almost see each of the stars in the milky way. Among those points of light is a darkness that sometimes feels infinite and inevitable, but now it feels as natural and necessary as exhaling is to breathing. The stars begin to rotate faster, but they are not circling the planet; they are circling you. With no sense of dizziness, the stars swirl up into a great funnel-shaped cloud above you, pulsing with the life and energy of all that is. Remaining seated, you look off into the middle distance toward the horizon, but you can feel the swirl of stars above you as a tingle in your scalp. It swirls faster than imagination, but the point of the funnel moves languidly, as if through water; slowly, it reaches the crown of your head. When it touches, you feel a warmth and love enter your mind and brain, traveling through your nerves outward to each of your organs from your bones to your skin, causing each of your cells to glow with an inner light. You are made of the universe, and its light is your own light. The contact ends, the stars slow their circling, and return to their positions in the sky. You look up again and know that you have returned to your original surroundings. Take three slow breaths, and as you release the third open your eyes, stretching your body when you are ready.

◄§ EXERCISE ﬞ§►
Guided Meditation: The Owl's Flight

What you'll do:

Settle into a comfortable position and begin meditating. Arrange with a friend to begin reading the following, or record yourself reading it ahead of time to play now. In the alternative, study the following paragraph with care, and allow it to unfold before your mind's eye as you meditate. Keep your physical eyes closed.

You are aware of a sort of darkness around you. It is not new. Sometimes it clouds your vision and freezes you with uncertainty, but at other times it recedes to just beyond the corner of your eye.

It is time to pierce that darkness. Take a deep breath, and feel air slightly chilled by the night enter your lungs. As you release that breath, you become aware that you are perched on a branch, your strong talons holding you fast. You take a look around, your wide eyes taking in detail and especially movement. With no moon to be seen, the forest before you is drenched in light. Tiny insects zip from leaf to leaf through the air, while others walk on the bark of the tree. Above you, bats flit back and forth, snatching airborne bugs up with their mouths. Stretching your wings, you take silently to the air, the bats deftly avoiding you as you circle around to a nearby meadow. The small mammals are dark blots against the dark ground, but you know that darkness is but an illusion, and everywhere there is light. Your pass above the meadow confirms that there are many mice below, unaware of your presence because you are a dark blot against a starless sky. You are no mouse, though; in this moment you are the owl, and you know that darkness is but an illusion. You circle the meadow twice more before alighting briefly on a rock. The rock grounds you to your human body, and you let out a soft owl's cry before again becoming aware of yourself and the lessons you learned from the owl's flight. When you are ready, open your eyes and take a stretch to help yourself fully return to your body.

The above guided meditation is inspired by shapeshifting, an advanced form of ritual magic that involves possession by or shifting consciousness into an animal. Kirk White has a detailed script for a shapeshifting ritual in the book *Advanced Circle Magick*.[40]

---

40. Kirk White, *Advanced Circle Magick: Essential Spells and Rituals for Every Season* (New York: Citadel Press, 2007), 174–82.

Shadow Work

Carl Jung was the one who popularized the idea that each of us has a "shadow self," a place in our minds where we suppress those parts of our personality that we learned in our youth must be hidden if we are to survive. This separation of aspects of the self is acknowledged in many cultures and traditions, although the specifics vary. One might speak of retrieving pieces of the soul that have been lost, or repairing the connection between heart and mind. Shadow work is that collection of techniques intended to reintegrate those hidden parts of the self, which otherwise can become triggered and cause unexpected behavior. Untangling what's hidden in the shadow can release some of what's making you into a comfortable place for depression to set up housekeeping.

Courtney Weber says that shadow work in witchcraft helps: "I was in a dark spot, trying talk therapy, and couldn't get out of the funk. I've always resisted taking medications, I never have. I don't deserve that."

"There's been a lot of shadow work that I've done which, whilst it hasn't specifically focused on depression, has shifted a lot of the underlying trauma," Siobhan Johnson told me. "Something that was initially a hard pill to swallow but has worked wonders since is the idea that if I don't have something that I want, I'm blocking it or rejecting it in some way."

As with most methods of real healing, shadow work is not a quick fix. It can take years to dredge up and accept those rejected parts of the self, and it can be as painful as setting a broken bone. Witches often undertake shadow work on their own, but some people find it's easier to engage your shadow self with a trusted companion, such as a therapist. When someone else is helping, they can ask questions to help direct your thoughts as described in this sample exercise.

❧ EXERCISE ❧
Shadow Work

What you'll do:

In this exercise, you will think about a person who gets under your skin. The goal is to allow the thoughts and feelings to rise up so that you can observe them and acknowledge how—and why—this person affects you as they do.

1. Take a few moments to relax your body and mind into a meditative state.
2. When you are ready, think or say aloud the name of a person who really bothers you.
3. Take some time to think about this person's most irritating qualities.
4. Now, name any of those traits that you sometimes exhibit.
5. What changes in you when this person is around? What traits and qualities emerge?
6. How do you feel about the parts of you that are reflected back by this terribly annoying person?

Now, take some time to talk through what you're thinking and feeling with your therapist or other partner, or reflect on it privately in a journal entry, to aid in integrating what you have discovered. When you're ready to wind up this exercise, take a few minutes to release these thoughts and feelings, ground the excess emotional energy, and center yourself through meditation.

Shadow work can be used to connect with parts of the self that are deeply hidden. This exercise is just a beginning. There are many excellent books available that explore this process more deeply.

In the Company of Spirits

It's not always easy to find ways to live in community with other humans when experiencing depression. Fortunately pagans have other options open to us, in addition to human company. Other companions may include domestic animals, nature spirits, ancestors, other spirits, and gods. Any and all of these can and, in my opinion, should be part of one's community, but *humans should be as well*. If you are in a place where that does not seem possible, don't fixate on it, but know that the company of one's own form of life is important. Other humans might feel completely alien, but through a combination of evolution and cultural indoctrination we all understand something about connecting to one another that cannot always be explained in words. As Courtney Weber observed, "We are not cougars, we are not solo creatures. We're wolves. We're pack animals."

Feeling at home in a place is to be attuned with the spirit of that place. Kari Tauring shared how a sense of "home" promotes healing: "The water we are drinking makes our bodies," she said. "All of my water is from the Mississippi River," and she finds she notes its absence when she travels, even to her ancestral Norway where the sense of belonging runs deep in her. "Back home, in my little house in Minnesota on the Mississippi, I have that full-body sense of belonging. This is the water I drink, the food I eat, the air I breathe, the microbes getting into my bloodstream." There is a very real chemical change that occurs from drinking water in a new place, and Tauring said it takes about seven years to become fully "of" the new locale. From that point on, "that is your healing space." One can feel ancestral or past-life connections and longings that make one feel immediately at home in an otherwise unfamiliar place, as well. Regardless of how it comes about, "The point is to find the place that puts you in that *hug*-like, playful, delighted space," which is where healing of the spirit can occur. If that space is also in nature, so much the better.

Your home, your place of belonging, is full of spirits, including some that happen to have a corporeal form. We are always in the company of spirits, but it's the spirits we seek out and intentionally build relationships with who are most going to help with healing.

Who belongs in that company of spirits? Here are some options:

- **Pets** and other other animals. I have already spoken about the many animals that are always in residence at Kirk White's Laurelin Retreat Center. My own life could be described as a series of relationships with cats. During my most difficult period there was more than 400 miles of distance between me and the cat I considered my familiar. I was living in my college town and didn't have the resources to care for my Biff there. A roommate took in a friend's pregnant cat when that person moved away, and one of those kittens bonded with me, but finding a rental space for humans and cats proved impossible and I had to re-home sweet Arthur. I'd been more than a year without any animal companions by the time I hit rock bottom. I'd long thought that it was best to be far from any beloved animals during that time, but now I see another possibility: that their presence can make life easier in some ways. Research done during the early months of the pandemic in the United States supports that position, suggesting that pets are a source of considerable emotional support.[41]

---

41. Ratschen, Elena, Emily Shoesmith, Lion Shahab, Karine Silva, Dimitra Kale, Paul Toner, Catherine Reeve, Daniel S. Mills. "Human-animal relationships and interactions during the Covid-19 lockdown phase in the UK: Investigating links with mental health and loneliness." Plos One: September 25, 2020. https://doi.org/10.1371/journal.pone.0239397.

- **Nature spirits** is a category that might include any physical being found in nature (such as trees and wild animals, but also rocks and rivers and flowers), as well as aspects of nature that don't have an obvious physical form, weather phenomena from breezes to storms, for example, as well as beings that are called fairies and wights, among other words. It is beyond the scope of this book to dig into the ways to attune to local land spirits, but I will say this: when in depression and beginning such relationships, keep it simple and keep it hyper-local. Remember how Orion Foxwood's mother would simply spend time with the plants in the garden. Don't become the self-appointed protector of a forest preserve to start; try sitting with your back against the tree that is closest to your front door. If stillness doesn't suit you, there is a technique I would use when I was primarily a gaiaped: walk a wooded path or trail, and touch the trees that are in reach as you pass. This is a gentle way to gradually come into communion with a larger wooded area, albeit without the same level of commitment as that self-appointed protector position might carry. Leaving an offering for your local spirits is a common way to build this relationship; a little milk or honey in a bowl on the windowsill is one way to do this. As with all offerings, remember to clean the dish out after no more than a day. Small steps are positive steps. It's always possible to take several steps in quick succession.

◆§ EXERCISE §◆
Sitting in Nature

What you'll need:

- clothing that's suitable for the weather, and something to sit on if the ground isn't suitable.
- a journal or other means to reflect upon the experience.

What you'll do:

1. Find a place to sit outside where other humans are unlikely to interrupt you. It's fine if there are humans around, as they are as part of the natural world as everything else.

2. Have a seat and allow yourself a few minutes just to breathe naturally as your body relaxes. You might lean against a tree, or climb one, or find a comfortable patch of grass, or a favorite sun-warmed stone, or a spot on the bank of a river or the shore of the ocean. What's important is to be outside, under the sky instead of a roof.

3. Close your eyes and listen to the sounds around you. Some may be human language or machinery, and these may draw your focus, but allow yourself to hear all the sounds as one, including that of your own breathing.

4. Open your eyes and take in the scene. Do not look at any object or detail; leave the focus of your eyes in the middle distance and try to get the sense that you're seeing everything through peripheral vision only.

5. Place your hands upon the ground and, using touch alone, try to learn something about the earth that supports you. If you're unable to reach to the ground, reach for a living plant and explore it without destroying it.

6. Open your mind and senses to the world around you and, if you're led, write something in your journal that is inspired by the spirits around you.

- **Ancestors** can be really intimidating to work with, but that's because many of us make the mistake of just thinking about dead family members we knew in life. That's a good place to start for genealogy, which can certainly inform an ancestor practice, but it's not always the best way to begin honoring one's ancestors. By some definitions, anyone we knew in life is not an ancestor at all—these are the beloved dead, who have not yet gained the perspective of an ancestor. It's sometimes easier to get one's mind around dead people if we have a name and a picture associated with them, but the vast majority of family ancestors lived before there were cameras, and little if anything about their lives will ever be known to us. I actually avoid using any pictures in my ancestor shrine to remind me of this very fact. Fortunately, *none of this has much to do with ancestor veneration.* Everything I just described comes from a place of life privilege, and presumes that the dead have the same priorities as the living. Names, deeds, and likenesses are tools created by the living to remember people who are no longer living. There is little evidence that the dead actually care about any of these trappings of mortal existence, and it's a shame to allow problematic relationships with people we knew in life to stand in the way of connecting with that long line of people without whom we would not be alive at all. Ancestor veneration can instead focus on the uncounted generations of ancestors who contributed to one's existence. We can ask that they walk with us, shore us up, share wisdom and coping mechanisms for similar life challenges (including depression), and affirm that we have value if for no other reason than by bearing their genetics into the present day. The Norse concept of *orlog*, as explained by Kari Tauring, suggests that illness has a lineage and that by naming that lineage we can negotiate with the illness directly. One does not have to know that specific, named ancestors experienced depression for this to be important; trust that some of the stress borne by your ancestors and passed down for you to carry has worn away your resistance and made it easier for depression to slip in. Our ancestors offer their resilience, their weakness, their acceptance, their resistance. Their spirits and the spirit of depression have danced full life cycles together, and no secrets or fears remain. There is no darkness darker than death, and death holds no fear for the dead.

This is also explored in family constellation therapy, "which was founded by a German therapist named Bert Hellinger," and "focuses on the hidden role of ancestors in shaping our lives and works to help us make peace with these ghost-like presences."[42] This is something we can ask our ancestors to aid us with, both the naming and the negotiating. Who better to help negotiate than those who wish us well, but whose burdens we often still carry?

Engaging with dead people we knew in life is much more advanced work that is part necromancy and part therapy. One reason they are qualitatively different is because when a person dies, that precise self of that living person is no more. At the very least, the body—which is

---

42. Pollan, *How to Change Your Mind*, 256.

part of our identity as human beings—is lost. If it is true that emotions emerge from the body, then someone without a body is not going to experience emotion in the way that we living experience them. There may be memories of love and hate, anger and happiness that are very strong, but they will not be accompanied by changes to respiration and heart rate, temperature and pupil size. I see my connection to the people I knew in life—parents and grandparents—as a bridge between myself and my ancestors. My ancestors are people whose lives shaped the foundation of my own, but died before my birth. They have no memories of holding me in their arms, and their interest in my well-being has different motivations. I never felt grief at their passing because they were dead before I knew how to grieve. The wisdom and healing I can access through my ancestors is not filtered through life experience, and represents a completely different perspective than what I gain from my more recently dead relatives.

This concept of ancestors is focused on the family tree, but that's not to suggest that genetics is tied to ancestry. My stepchild has every right to claim my ancestors. Anyone adopted into a family is part of that family and all of its ancestors. The priests in my temple consider all the prior priests of our gods to be ancestors, and heroes are often considered ancestors of entire peoples because of the influence they have had. Do not allow another to define for you who may be named an ancestor, unless that ancestor agrees. As with many spiritual matters, divination and discernment are important tools for answering these questions, and they are tools that are much less effective when used in solitude.

❧ EXERCISE ❧
Letter to an Ancestor

What you'll need:

- stationery, a post card, or paper, as well as a writing implement.
- envelope (optional).

What you'll do:

1. Find a spot with good light and a solid writing surface where you can sit undisturbed.

2. Have a seat, close your eyes, and allow yourself to breathe naturally.

3. Visualize your parents standing behind you, each with a hand upon your shoulder. If you have other parental figures in your life, you may find them standing in for, or beside, your biological parents. Feel the weight of those hands upon your shoulders, expressing support.

4. Continue to breathe naturally, and with each exhalation visualize additional generations: your grandparents with hands upon the shoulders of your parents, great-grandparents' hands upon grandparents shoulders. If you were to turn around you could not count all the people standing in succession, each supporting the next generation, all supporting you. All your ancestors, stretching back through the mists of time, are with you.

5. Without opening your eyes, ask aloud or silently if there is one among your ancestors who wishes to help you now. Wait until you sense a positive response. You may receive a name or picture a face, but this is not common.

6. Open your eyes and write a letter to this ancestor. Ask about their struggles and challenges. Ask if they have ever experienced depression and describe your own experience in as much detail as you are willing. Share your fears and anxieties.

7. Sign and date the letter, and fold it up. If you wish, seal it in an envelope.

8. Place the letter under your head the next time you sleep and be open to receiving a response in your dreams. We do not remember most of our dreams in our conscious mind, but an answer will be received.

9. If you do recall anything of your dreams, try to write down your impressions upon awakening.

10. You may destroy the letter later if you wish, or keep it in a safe place so that you or your own descendants will have a record of your journey.

- **Other spirits** can certainly be part of one's community. Not every person is associated with an aspect of nature or is an ancestor by genealogy or choice. For example, Hellenic tradition speaks of the agathos daimon, the good spirit that helps to provide opportunity, facilitate luck, and ensure that signs are neither missed nor misinterpreted. Witches and magicians sometimes refer to the "higher self" that is an aspect of the individual; I daresay that parts of oneself that are distinct enough that we do not automatically know their thoughts and motivations should probably be included in one's community, and thus might fit in here. The caution I offer is about spirits that are unfamiliar to other humans in one's life, because a being without a body has certain advantages when it comes to being misleading about its nature and motivations. Spirit work is also beyond the scope of this book and should not be undertaken without training. Stick to those spirits already vetted within your religious or esoteric tradition if you lack that training, and especially don't go introducing yourself to unfamiliar spirits during a period of depression without some friends along.

- **Gods** are a tricky bunch at any time, and depression is no different. Even those of us who have cultivated close relationships with particular deities find them going silent for periods of time, and that can feel really awful when it coincides with depression. It could be unrelated, or it could be that the god is providing support in ways you cannot detect (which an unknown Christian attempted to describe in the poem *Footprints*). Some gods will be more present during depression; Joshua Tenpenny described such a relationship with Hela. From my own experience, I know that my life is fuller and more stable because I choose to maintain a regular practice honoring certain gods without fail, whether I feel a presence or not. I do not make offerings with an expectation of anything in return, and usually that is exactly what I get. However, my life is full of blessings, even when I fail to recognize them as such. I only number a handful (well, a double-handful, maybe an armful) of gods as part of my community, and I feel honored that they wish to be included.

- **Living human beings** are part of any complete community. I understand that this can be a big problem for someone experiencing depression. The mind wants you to withdraw from the field, not advance. The thought of interacting with other humans can trigger stress, anxiety, and fear. At the same time, depression can result in behaviors that are specifically *anti*-social, like outbursts of anger and expressions of awkwardness. Sometimes we feel unwelcome because the voice of depression is trying to get us alone, but other times we feel unwelcome because we really *are* unwelcome due to depression-inspired acts. Poor attention to hygiene, weight gain or loss due to an altered relationship with food, or even a sense that you're not "all there" because of brain fog or poor sleep habits can all contribute to others feeling uncomfortable in your presence. Humans can also give off cold pricklies when they are confronted with someone whose body or brain functions differently than what is expected, as well as people who have diseases with obvious physical symptoms. Quite a bit of social justice work deals with trying to mitigate or eliminate these kinds of reactions. Resolving those societal issues is beyond the scope of this book, but it's important to be aware that they exist, fair or not.

◆§ EXERCISE §◆
Tending a Depression Shrine

This longer-term project is to create and use a shrine as a way to engage with depression as a spirit.

What you'll need:

- Three coins of the same denomination; these will be your depression divination coins and will be used to communicate with the spirit of depression, as well as for asking other questions related to the condition. If the three coins you select are also minted in your birth year, this fact will help them attune to you, but it's not a necessity. You can always replace coins in the set with some minted in your birth year as you come upon them.

- An offering bowl.
- An opaque container with a covering, which can be as simple as another bowl with some aluminum foil to close the top, or a coffee can, gift box, or a basket with a cloth. All it needs to be is darker on the inside when it's closed.
- Candle holder and candle, or an LED that looks like a candle.
- A spool of black thread.
- Offerings for the spirit: I use wine, but another edible food or drink should be acceptable. In time, you will ask the spirit directly what it prefers.
- Shaving from an exposed tree root (optional).

What you'll do:

Step one: Identify a location.

Pick a spot in your living space that you will see every day, but that won't become an obstacle to others living in the same place. Clear off a space on a bookshelf, windowsill, dresser top, corner of a desk, or space on a kitchen counter. If communicating with housemates is not enough to help select a spot, divination may help. Here's a sub-exercise for that purpose.

❧ EXERCISE ❧
Divining a Location for Your Depression Shrine

What you'll do:

1. Narrow down your choices using the criteria in step one: identify a location.

2. At each of the potential locations, flip your depression divination coins while asking: "Is this the preferred location for my depression shrine?" Record the number of coins that land heads up.

3. The location with the most number of heads is where you should site the shrine. If there is a tie, do another round of coin tosses for those locations only, repeating until there is no longer a tie.

Direct these questions to the universe, or the gods that oversee divination in your tradition, or your patron deity, or your ancestors, or the spirit of depression itself. You may not be ready to engage directly with this spirit just yet, but you will be.

Step two: Assemble the depression shrine.

The basic layout of the shrine is simple: Place the offering bowl and the candle side by side, and put the container either between them in a line or behind them, so they form a triangle. That's all you need. You may wish to add more, such as an altar cloth under the objects, but simple is fine and shrines tend to grow with time. Trust your intuition as to what and when to add to it.

Step three: Create a depression totem.

It's time to make a physical form for the spirit to inhabit, and invite it in.

To begin making the totem, sit before the shrine and take a few moments to center yourself. When you are ready, take the container, remove the covering, and hold it in your lap or hand. Turn your awareness inward, and seek out and focus on a symptom of depression to help bring the feelings to the surface. When this becomes uncomfortable, visualize pouring some of that feeling into the container as you break a length of thread from the spool. Say, "Spirit of depression, you have tangled me up, but I would like to offer you something else to tangle." Roll the thread between thumb and fingers, place it in the container, and cover it up. Place an offering in the bowl and say, "Spirit of depression, I am making for you this fine home. If you move from me to this place I will honor your sacrifice with offerings such as this." Light the candle and say, "May this light fill the hole in my heart from your leaving me, spirit of depression. Know that I will be well if you free yourself from me." Remain quietly at the shrine until you feel ready, then extinguish the candle and withdraw.

From this point on, repeat this next series of steps to build the totem. These steps can be repeated at whatever frequency you wish. If you don't work on the totem at least once a day, though, remember that offerings usually should not be left more than twenty-four hours before disposal.

1. Dispose of offerings by leaving them outside, placing them in a compost bin, or by wrapping and placing them in the garbage; wash and dry the offering bowl.

2. Sit before the shrine and center yourself.

3. Pick up the totem container and open it.

4. Awaken the spirit of depression within you by focusing on a current symptom, then direct it into the container.

5. Break a length of thread from the spools and say, "Spirit of depression, you have tangled me up, but I would like to offer you something else to tangle in the form of this fine, new home."

6. Pick up the totem and tie the new piece of thread to it, creating a tendril. Pass it through or around other threads, if you feel that leading.

7. Pour or place a new offering in the bowl and say, "Spirit of depression, I am making for you this fine home. If you move from me to this place I will honor your sacrifice with offerings such as this."

8. Light the candle and say, "May this light fill the hole in my heart from your leaving me, spirit of depression. Know that I will be well if you free yourself from me."

9. Remain quietly at the shrine until you feel ready, then close the totem container, extinguish the candle, and withdraw.

If you have collected a shaving from an exposed tree root, this can be added during any cycle. These root shavings are good for tangling things up,[43] and I find it works as well as setting a candle in the holder with melted wax. Just tie one of the totem's tendrils around the bit of root, making it part of the totem. Tie later threads wherever it makes sense, as the root is now as much a tendril as the threads.

You might be led to include other small items, such as beads that represent loved ones who have suffered due to your experience of depression. As long as the object is durable, has signifi-

---

43. Ballard, Byron. *Staubs and Ditchwater: A Friendly and Useful Introduction to Hillfolks' Hoodoo.* Asheville, North Carolina: Silver Rings Press, 2012, 59.

cance, can be attached to the totem, and is added with intent, just trust your gut on what to include.

The attractiveness of the totem as a home for this spirit can be enhanced by juicing up the individual threads. Here are some variations that may speak to your condition:

- **Alcohol:** If you are able to be around alcohol, or you have some on hand that you probably shouldn't, dip a thread in it and say, "Spirit of depression, you have bottled me up, but I wish to give this [type of alcohol] back to you." This variant would also be suitable if alcohol has influenced the lives of any of your family or ancestors.

- **Saliva:** Moisten the thread in your mouth and say, "Spirit of depression, you have taken the spit out of me, but I am now giving you my spit willingly. Come take up residence in this fine, new home."

- **Urine:** Moisten however is most convenient and say, "Spirit of depression, you have taken the piss out of me, but I am now giving it to you willingly. Come take up residence in this fine, new home."

- **Sweat:** Collect as appropriate and apply to the thread, saying, "Spirit of depression, you have brought the sweat of fear and anxiety upon me. I give you my sweat willingly and say: the danger for me will pass if you would but take up residence in this fine, new home."

- **Blood:** This can be reserved for when you are already bleeding. Moisten the thread and say, "Spirit of depression, you have been in my blood since it was in the veins of my ancestors. Take this offering of my precious blood and take up residence in this fine, new home."

- **Tears:** Wipe the thread in your tears and say, "Spirit of depression, through you I know sadness before all else. Take these tears and the weight of your sadness and come live in this fine, new home."

If other personal concerns or fluids come to mind, follow the same pattern as in these examples to include them.

You can stop adding on to your depression totem when it feels like it is starting to fill up the container. Since it's entirely or very nearly entirely thread, it could take some time for it to reach that point. As it grows, you may find that it becomes more uncomfortable to sit with the container open. This means that the container is starting to be filled with the depression spirit. If you find yourself either a) unsure if the totem is getting physically too big for the container or b) unwilling to open the container and look upon it, then your totem is probably as big as it needs to be.

If you feel you need confirmation, flip your depression divination coins and ask if the spirit of depression is ready to move into the totem. Three heads is an enthusiastic yes. If the response falls short, either ask again the next time you come to the shrine, or ask follow-up questions to determine if you need to adjust the frequency of your visits or the type of offerings. For these responses, three heads is a clear yes, three tails a strong no, and two of one or the other is leaning in that direction.

Step four: Maintaining the depression shrine.

The depression totem and shrine are intended to be an inviting place to live for a spirit that is used to getting attention. Convincing it to reside there full-time takes time and effort—in other words, attention.

With a depression shrine set up, it becomes easier to engage with the spirit of depression. The depression divination coins can be used to ask questions about the type and frequency of offerings it desires, as described in step three. This is a spirit that asks a lot to appease it, but every relationship with a spirit is a negotiation, and what it asks for the first time around isn't necessarily the minimum it will accept.

During this ongoing tending phase, continue to use the candle as a reminder of the love and life that fills that part of yourself that's no longer taken up by the spirit of depression.

A depression shrine is also a physical symbol of your relationship with depression. Over time, maintaining the shrine can begin to feel tiresome, and it may become neglected. Since the spirit of depression desires your attention, rest assured that if the shrine becomes dusty, disorganized, or overlooked, then the spirit has likely relocated back into you, and you will have to clean it up and begin making offerings again to entice the spirit to return. Depression coming in cycles may already be familiar, but this exercise allows you to negotiate as a way to take control of the cycle and encourage the spirit to move back out of you again. Failing to tend the shrine is not what causes the depression to return to you; rather, it's a warning that this has already occurred, one more way to recognize this shift. When you realize you've been neglecting the shrine, try to restart the habit of logging your moods as a way to confirm your condition.

In time, you may want to try asking other questions using the depression divination coins, such as its purpose in your life. Despite the devastating consequences of depression, I've come to realize that this spirit's intentions are not malevolent. In deepening the relationship, I hope to reach an understanding that intentions don't matter as much as the results, and to find a way toward restorative justice.

Tending a depression shrine is not a substitute for other practices, such as meditation, prayer, participating in community, therapy, and medication. Some or all of these will always be part of maintaining healthy boundaries between you and the spirit of depression. The shrine allows for those boundaries to have a tangible marker, though, putting physical distance between yourself and depression.

Divination During Depression

Practicing divination from within depression can feel like shouting into the void. The depression divination coins that are described as part of the tending a depression shrine are useful to communicating with the spirit directly, but that's a very limited scope. Divination for oneself is fraught with difficulty under the best of circumstances, but during depression it's largely an opportunity to draw the least favorable conclusions while interpreting a reading. This is an opportunity to get readings from another person.

Acknowledging Depression

In addition to isolating ourselves, one of the behaviors we often assume during depression is simply denying the condition entirely. Speaking about it can bring a sense of shame, and even thinking about it is uncomfortable. Accepting your relationship with depression is a valuable step toward transforming it.

Johnson believes that "listening to one's depression/anxiety without judgement or accepting what it says at face value, is the most important part of healing. All your depression wants is for you to be safe, and not hurt, and when that makes you too numb it asks you to be hurt to try and wake you up. Your shadow is confused, it has all the best and all the worst of you and is just trying to love you in the best way it can."

Perhaps the most profound wisdom Orion Foxwood shared is that if one does "sit in the authenticity of the place you are, and speak straight from that mystery, you have more presence."

The ability to deny is one of the most awesome powers of the human mind, but here it is used in service of the spirit of depression. In effect, it's much like a freezing spell that's used to still the tongue against speaking out. To be ready to sit in the authenticity of the place you are, you must be willing to free that stagnant energy, to thaw that freeze. Depression uses our own strength against us, so the question to ask is how you are blocking yourself from acknowledging the presence of depression, and who can help you clear that barrier?

Purification

As meditation is to the mind, and washing is to the body, purification is to the spirit. Regularly using a purification method to cleanse the aura and clear away spiritual clutter can be just as beneficial as keeping the sink clear of dirty dishes. Depression thrives in the mental, spiritual, and physical clutter that we accumulate while experiencing depression; this is a relationship that grows because it feeds upon itself. Purify when you feel unworthy to use your altar, or when you feel guilty for neglecting an oath or promise, or when you feel like a bad person, or any time you feel like you need it.

⊰ EXERCISE ⊱
Purification with Water

What you'll need:

- a bowl of water.
- a match.

What you'll do:

1. Light the match and extinguish it in the water. You have now created *khernips*, an ancient Greek form of holy water, using the simplest of recipes.
2. Sprinkle some of the water upon yourself, or use it to wash your hands and face.
3. If there is any remaining, use it to wipe up dust or dirt on your altar or sacred objects.
4. Dispose of the remainder by pouring it outside.

⊰ EXERCISE ⊱
Purification with Smoke

What you'll need:

- a fireproof bowl.
- a bundle of sage or another dried herb that you use for purification.
- a lighter or matches.

What you'll do:

1. Light the sage, blowing on it as needed to make it smoulder.

2. Using your hands or another implement, waft smoke around your head and body, keeping the bowl ready to catch the ashes.

3. If there is any remaining, you may preserve it for later by putting some water in the bowl and extinguishing the sage, hanging it up to dry.

4. Use the water to wipe up dust or dirt on your altar or sacred objects.

5. Dispose of the ashes by leaving them under a plant or on bare earth outside.

◄§ EXERCISE §►
Purification with Scent

What you'll need:

- essential oils used for purification, such as sage, myrrh, or mullein, or an aromatherapy blend of purifying scents.
- a diffuser or other means to distribute the scent.

What you'll do:

1. Activate the diffuser and add the scents or oils as directed.

2. Sit or stand nearby, and allow the scent to enter your nostrils naturally.

3. Take several deep, cleansing breaths once you detect the scent. Fill your lungs to a slow count of four, hold the air in for a slow count of four, release to a slow count of four, and hold your lungs empty for a slow count of four.

4. If the gods or spirits of your tradition accept oils or aromatherapy scents as offerings, give some now. If your altar or sacred objects are dusty or disused, give them a quick wipe with a cloth to help reawaken them first.

⬖§ EXERCISE §⬖
Purification with Sound

What you'll need:

• a gong, bell, or tuning fork.

What you'll do:

1. Sound the instrument and move it slowly over and around your body, sounding again when you are no longer able to hear it. A tuning fork may only need to be struck once or twice, while a bell may need to be jingled constantly.
2. Once you have covered your entire body, allow yourself to fall into silence for at least one full minute.
3. Shake off any residual spiritual impurities by flicking your hands in the direction of an open door or window.
4. Take a moment to review your sacred space, and dust or reorganize it as needed.

⬖§ JOURNAL EXERCISE §⬖
List of Grievances

Set a timer for seven minutes.

Write down all the ways that you feel you have suffered due to depression. As you write, visualize the words smouldering or catching fire from your feelings. Your list can include symptoms like stomach discomfort and headaches, or lethargy and irritability, but don't stop there. Jot down the times when you've declined social engagements or fell short on the job, relationships that have changed, and opportunities you've missed. You might imagine that you're building a case against depression and you're gathering evidence, or you could decide you're composing a complaint letter. However you frame it, don't hold back. Include anything you've ever blamed on depression.

Continue after the timer runs out if there are ideas that really need to come out. When you finish, close your journal and close your eyes. Visualize your journal, still smoking slightly from the power of your words, and imagine a slight chill coming over your body because of all the heat you expelled during this exercise. Sit quietly until your breathing and heartbeat feel like they have returned to a resting state.

eight
Rituals and Routine

It is easy during depression to decide to do nothing. The structure of life can fall away. Mindfully reestablishing routines can help order the day without it becoming overwhelming. With a set routine—in writing, if necessary—one need only focus on what's next, which can make it easier at times. A routine that includes ritual injects some sacredness into activities at a time when thoughts of magic or gods are far from mind.

Thought requires effort and energy, both of which can be in short supply at this time. Automatic actions, such as driving home along a familiar route or brushing teeth, can be accomplished without much thought at all: start the process, and it will unfold even if you're not paying attention to the details. New activities require a lot more attention, a lot more energy, than a familiar routine, which makes it more difficult to maintain during depression. The spirit of depression may try to break those habits with discouraging, negative self-talk, but stopping a rolling stone is not as easy as keeping a still one from moving in the first place.

When establishing new routines for myself, I find that infusing them with sacred context is helpful because thinking about gods and my role in their plans is very motivational for me. Others might not find it inspiring to dedicate cleaning the toilet to Cloacina, but establishing a personal routine of religious ritual and practice can be an important solace during periods of depression, even if you don't mix the mundane in quite so much as I. A daily practice is easiest to maintain because it's much harder to forget. Include it at the very beginning or end of your waking day to make it even easier.

Sometimes, all one can do is go through the motions. Treading water can mean the difference between life and death, and choosing life is my preference because I can only choose death the one time. For me, depression can result in time slipping away lying in bed or staring at a screen or listening to news reports while the world rolls on by. I have found it helpful to establish *routines* to ensure that I achieve a certain bare minimum each day even during difficult times. I also strongly recommend the use of *rituals* to help one find a path back to more balanced place.

In this context, I use the word "routine" to mean a behavior or set of behaviors that one performs regularly. Every day, I clean out the cat pans, refill the water bowl, and sweep up part of the house. After every meal, I brush and floss my teeth. Once a week, I take the recycling and garbage out. Two nights a week, I prepare dinner. These things all will get accomplished even if I were to experience depression as severe as it was for me in the early nineties, because I have established these routines. Routine can take time and effort to put into place, and I have used a combination of calendar reminders, strategically-placed sticky notes, and other cues to get them into my head. Muscle memory eventually takes over, especially for daily routines, and I find that *not* engaging in a given routine is more likely to catch my notice that actually performing it, once it's established.

Routine can certainly have a downside. Obsessive-compulsive disorder can be an expression of routine taken too far. Much of the experience of depression is a negative use of repetitive, routine thoughts and behaviors, such as watching hour after hour of television or sitting alone and dwelling on your own shortcomings. The difference is in the intent. No one plans to live a life in depression, except perhaps for the spirit of depression itself.

Witches and others who practice magic should be prepared to apply intention to their routines. Take some time to examine existing routines to determine if they are adding quality or value to one's life, and I'd wager that the ones that are not were either not created with intention, or that the intention and the routine have diverged since. It's perfectly acceptable to lay down routines that do not "spark joy," as Marie Kondo might say. If you feel that you are unable to lay down a routine despite wishing to, you may have more success with help from another person. Whether that person should be an acquaintance, a confidante, an authority figure, or a mental health professional will depend upon your circumstances.

Ritual is a collection of activities that might include gestures, words, and actions; when I refer to "ritual" I am referring to those activities used to further one's religion, which for pagans might include honoring gods, communing with spirits, or working magic, among other things. Ritual can be routine in the sense that it can be done on a regular schedule, but it can also feel routine in the sense that it's ordinary or pedestrian. This is something that can be hard to accept: Ritual will not always feel special, the gods do not always wish to break our heads open or even make their presence known, and at times it will not feel like there is any point to performing any kind of ritual. This can and does happen to every religious person at one time or another, even people who never experience depression, but it can feel especially harsh during a period of depression. I am here to tell you to do it anyway. If you're a member of a coven that meets on the full moon, join them on the full moon. If you bake and hand out cookies for noumenia like me, keep on baking. If people come to you for magical assistance, go ahead and provide it. Others I have interviewed in these pages confirm that ritual has value even they aren't feeling it because of depression. Courtney Weber said that she always feels better when she spends time at her altar, and Sarah W. affirms that returning to a spiritual practice always brings benefit. Weber and Ivo Dominguez, Jr. both confirm that one can perform magic as effectively as ever even if one can't feel the flow of energy— provided that one has trained and practiced all along. Gods can and do withdraw from our lives for reasons of their own, but depression seems to make it easier to believe one has been abandoned entirely. In my own experience, I have come to recognize that my patron especially has never left me, and in fact was especially supportive in times when I believed I was completely alone. Sarah W. speaks in this book about how Dionysos is present whether or not depression is being experienced, and Joshua Tenpenny speaks about a relationship with Hela that largely exists *only* during periods of depression. In the Hellenic context, part of the purpose of ritual is simply to thank the gods for their very existence and to make offerings while expecting nothing in return; this can be compared to just sending a friend a card or a text message because you're thinking of that person, rather than having an expectation of receiving something in return. Engage in ritual without expecting a miraculous intervention. You may get one anyway, but sometimes the work of the gods is less direct and overt than that. Ritual keeps the unseen as part of our community.

Ritual can be part of one's routine. I make offerings every morning to several gods and spirits, before I even have coffee for myself (which is a pretty big deal considering my deep and enduring relationship with Caffeina). That kind of ritual can bring the comfort of familiarity as well as strengthening relationships and esoteric skills. Ritual that is less frequent also tends to be more complex, which can easily feel overwhelming when one is experiencing depression. Whether one is capable of organizing and facilitating a more complex ritual is a personal decision, but consider including getting input from other humans who might be involved, or from non-humans by means of divination. I won't go deeply into divination here, but will say only that divination for oneself is dicey in the best of times, and during depression it should be done only with special caution, because the responses might end up reflecting back through depression rather than being answers sourced purely in spirit.

No matter what the ritual purpose, consider using an affirmation such as this before you begin:

> *I am a child of the gods, and the gods hear me*
> *even if I do not know their answer. I am a child of the universe,*
> *and the energy is within me even if I do not feel its release."*

Following are three rituals designed with depression in mind. The first is short and simple, something that can be performed every day. The other two are examples of more complex rituals, that draw upon Hellenic tradition.

◆§ EXERCISE §◆
A Simple Depression Ritual

What you'll need:

- nothing at all, but the rest of this list is optional.
- candle or an LED that looks like one.
- incense or potpourri that reminds you of a happy time.
- white noise or gentle background music set to play.

1. Set the tone: Light the candle, activate the scent, turn on the background sound, or simply find a comfortable seat. The only requirement is that you be still.

2. Center yourself: Sit with your back as upright as you can manage, and your feet on the floor if possible. Find balance for your body and allow your spirit to follow.

3. Open your mind: Breathe, deeply and slowly. Feel the air suffusing you with life as you inhale. As you exhale, feel your breath spreading out, to be taken in by some of the many plants that live alongside us.

4. Remember who you are: You are an essential part of the cycle. By your breath alone, you bring life to the world. With that baseline, all you do beyond that is magic.

5. Sit with this knowledge until you are called to another task.

It is done.

⋐§ EXERCISE §⋑
A Deipnon for Depression

Deipnon is a traditional Hellenic monthly feast for Hekate and the ancestors which takes place at the dark of the moon. It's intended to draw off miasma, which one might think of as spiritual grime that accumulates simply by living in the same way that dust and dirt piles up in any living space.

Give this ritual a thorough read before deciding if you want to try it. You can hold this meal just with your gods and ancestors, but meals are meant to be shared and humans tend to eat more than ancestors. If other humans join you, split up the tasks ahead of time. If you're the only human present, it's okay to pare back anything that feels too complicated. If you have a set of depression divination coins, you can use these to ask whether you should retain or remove any particular element.

What you'll need:

- white candle.
- moisture-resistant candle holder, or a fixative to hold the candle fast.
- depression totem.
- deipnon water: add portions of ouzo, garlic, celery, onion, salt, and olive oil to spring water and mix well.
- glass bowl.
- bowl for holding some form of blessed or holy water.
- one or two bowls for accepting offerings.
- wine or grape juice, or other liquid for libations.
- deipnon bread (biscuits covered with honey, cheese, peppermint, celery, onion, salt, and olive oil) or some other food offering.
- food for sharing with living humans (which may be of the same recipe, or not).
- slips of paper, from a pad or cut up from full-sized sheets, and a writing implement.

Altar Setup

Place this altar as low down as can be comfortably reached; the floor is not too low if kneeling or stooping down is not a problem. If you've set up a depression shrine, feel free to use that for this ritual.

Clean the space, at a minimum wiping away dust. Cover with a cloth if desired; you may choose a color that represents depression for you. I like bluish-black.

Add a white candle and a bowl of water that is suitable for purification in your tradition. A simple way to make khernips (the Hellenic lustral water) is to pour some clean water into a bowl, light a match, and extinguish it in the water. Another way is to add a pinch of salt to the clean water and ask Poseidon's blessing. This is one prayer I use to purify with salt:

> *Poseidon, keeper of the vast seas,*
> *I invoke your name of purity.*
> *Katharsios, with salt I cast to thee*
> *so mixed with water, khernips be.*

Any other way you traditionally prepare water for purification or ablution will work just as well.

If you have created a depression totem, place it below or beside the altar you've prepared, unless you're using a depression shrine; in that case, just leave it be.

Procession

In Hellenic practice, the *pompe* (procession) is an important part of any ritual. As someone who has also been a member of a Wiccan coven, I see some of its functions as overlapping with those of casting a circle—it aids with transition into sacred space, among other things. Unlike casting a circle, a procession doesn't require one to already be able to focus when one begins. At the same time, moving the body is good for mood and bad for depression.

Therefore, begin the ritual with a procession, even if that means walking no farther than across the living room or around to the other side of the bed. If you can work out a longer route, make it so. My first Hellenic ritual was a torch-lit procession through acres of woods to make offerings at several permanent shrines. I was exhausted by the time it was over, but apparently those gods took notice and it's been to my benefit. No matter the length of the procession, this is a time to get into the head-space of ritual and enter into *hieri siopi*, sacred silence, for the entire period. During Hellenic ritual stray words might be inadvertent omens, which is why participants are encouraged to "reserve your tongues for the holy" and avoid unnecessary chatter.

Purification

Conduct the *archesthai* (purification) of participants and altar at the end of the procession. If you're using khernips, sprinkle some over the altar and each person with fingers or, if you want to get fancy, a bay or laurel branch with leaves still attached. If you're using another method, follow best practices for that method.

Hearth-Blessing

In the tradition followed in Temenos Oikidios, Hestia is honored as goddess of the hearth in all rituals. To simplify things a bit, I'm suggesting a prayer that also invokes Hekate, as this is her feast.

Light the candle and say:

> *I bring my fire to the hearth of Hestia.*
> *I ask that this candle be as revealing a light,*
> *as that of torch-bearing Hekate*
> *who searched for lost Persephone.*

Place the candle and holder in the glass bowl, or affix it to the bottom. Make sure it's stable, because you're going to be walking around holding this.

Offerings

Deipnon is a time to dispose of the remains of old offerings, such as bits of matchsticks and incense, and as Sarah W. said in her interview, "I also give her intangible things I want to be rid of, like a feeling, that I also leave at a crossroads." In this instance, you will be gathering items to leave at a crossroads, asking Hekate to dispose of them.

Take up the pieces of paper in your hands and think about the feelings and experiences that are weighing you down in depression. You may wish to write key words on the slips of paper, but that's not necessary. What's most important is to allow yourself to feel them, to acknowledge them and their power over you, and to ask Hekate, in any words you choose, to take them from you. Set these and any remains of old offerings in a bowl.

Add some of the deipnon bread or other food offering. First cut a piece for Hestia, and say, "With this cut, I begin the sacrifice," setting it in the bowl. Put a full portion in for Hekate, saying this or other suitable words:

> *Mistress of the crossroads,*
> *who walks unchallenged in all lands,*
> *accept if you will this humble offering*
> *and carry my burdens to where they will do no harm.*

Take another portion, for the ancestors, and say:

> *Blood of my blood,*
> *bone of my bone,*
> *spirit of my spirit:*
> *may you share my burdens*
> *even as I share these offerings.*

Libations

A libation is a liquid offering, usually one that humans can drink, but olive oil and the like may be used as well. Pour out libations first to Hestia, then Hekate, and finally to the ancestors. In the Hellenic tradition I follow, libations and food offerings to underworld deities and the dead are not shared with the living (and Hestia is an underworld deity in this context). If burning is the plan, use a second bowl unless you're offering a flammable alcohol.

Cleansing of the Home

Take the prepared deipnon water and pour it into the glass bowl, into which you've already placed that lit candle. You're going to be carrying this about, so keep in mind that you don't want it sloshing over the edges or putting out the flame if you can help it. (If either of these occurs, do not take it as a bad omen; during depression people can be fatigued or clumsy, and things happen. Clean up, relight the candle, and pick up where you left off.)

Carry the bowl to every corner of the inside of your home or living space that you can reach, and visualize the light of the candle penetrating walls and floorboards as necessary to pierce any area of darkness you cannot. As you proceed, say this or similar words:

Away, away, shadows of the mind,
away, away, cobwebs of the soul.

Torch-bearing Hekate will walk with you and help collect the emotional baggage and triggers that have accumulated in your living space, the ones that reinforce and support depression. These will be collected and stored in the deipnon water.

Once the circuit is complete, return to the altar with the bowl. Snuff the candle and remove it. Add to this the remains of past offerings, and those emotional offerings that you collected on pieces of paper. Take this to the center of the nearest crossroads— two roads or paths that intersect at right angles—and dump the mess right in the middle. Turn around and immediately walk away, not looking back.

Feasting with the Gods

Upon your return, take some time to sit and eat with the gods, the ancestors, and whatever human and other companions are present. This is called *theoxenia*. Eat, drink, and strive to allow yourself to feel merry if you're able. When the meal is concluded, pour a final libation to Hestia.

Dispose of the libations and food offerings outside if you are able, or by wrapping them in a paper towel to place in the garbage if you are not.

It is finished.

⋘§ EXERCISE §⋙
Ritual Appeal to the Anemoi

The anemoi are gods of the wind in Hellenic mythology, who sometimes have emotions associated with them. This ritual is an appeal to the winds for aid in disrupting the obsessive self-reflection that can occur during a period of depression. If you wish to simplify this due to lack of support and spoons, read through it all first. Divination is a good way to find out what the gods will accept in this moment: Try asking about a component of the ritual and flipping the depression divination coins you gathered while making a depression shrine, or another three coins of your choosing. If all three come up heads then it's a clear yes, three tails are a definite no, and two of either leaning either positive or negative.

Feel free to invite other humans to participate; it will give more hands to carry items to the altar during the procession.

Items needed for the full ritual:

- images of the winds as depicted in antiquity or drawn yourself (statues of these gods might be even better, but these are hard to come by).
- one or more fans, scarves, pieces of stiff cardboard, or other items that will generate a breeze when waved.
- incense.
- a bowl of water.
- a dish of natural salt.
- barley.
- wine (mixed ahead of time with an equal amount of water; alternatively, pure water is also acceptable).
- animal crackers.
- bowl for offerings.

Altar Setup

Items can be brought in during the procession, but not so much as to load any one person down. The animal crackers and fans should be part of the procession. Any items not in the procession should be arranged on the altar ahead of time. Trust your intuition or lay items out in a simple grid.

Procession

Approach the altar waving fans or other items to move the air. Burning incense might be included for the purposes of blowing it about. The longer a procession you can manage, the more you will be able to shift into the mindset of being in the presence of the gods for a sacred ritual.

Purification and Offering of Barley

Take three pinches of salt and place it in the water, invoking one of the names of Poseidon to purify it:

> *Poseidon, keeper of the vast seas,*
> *I invoke your name of purity.*
> *Katharsios, with salt I cast to thee*
> *so mixed with water, khernips be.*

Sprinkle some of this *khernips* on yourself and any other participants.

You and anyone else particiating takes a small amount of barley, stands before the altar, and says:

> *I [include name if you wish] stand humbly before the gods,*
> *and offer this barley.*

Put the barley in the offering bowl.

Turn your palms upward to greet these gods of the sky and read:

> *Holy anemoi, progeny of bright Eos and Astraios of the boundless night,*
> *if we/I have ever poured a libation to you or done you service,*
> *hear me/us now.*

> *Frosty Boreas, matchless in strength and temper,*
> *Zephyrus, who knows love and loss in good measure,*
> *Fiery Notus, feared by farmers for good reason,*
> *and all the winds named and unnamed,*
> *accept these offerings to be made.*

> *As the winds bring storms and calm,*
> *do the anemoi roil the spirit in turn.*
> *Holy gods, if you are willing,*
> *allow calm thought and reason to pierce the clouds of the mind*
> *of all gathered before this altar at this time.*

Offerings and Libation

Select one of the animal crackers and cut off the back leg with a knife, saying:

> *With this cut, I begin the sacrifice.*

Place it in the offering bowl and consume the rest of it. All participants should put crackers in the bowl, retaining one each for eating themselves.

Now pour some of the wine atop the other offerings—a libation—saying:

> *I have poured a libation to you, I am pouring a libation to you,*
> *I will pour libations to you.*

Other participants should also add a small libation.

Other Ritual Actions

Say:

> *Holy anemoi, we thank you for your presence and pray*
> *for your guidance in clearing our minds of unwelcome thoughts.*
> *Accept this whistling in your honor.*

Now whistle a happy tune, as best you can, as you leave the ritual area by the same route you came. If you cannot whistle, use a breathy hum. Don't worry about whether it's in tune or not; it is the sincerity of the offering, not its perfection, that matters here.

⋘ JOURNAL EXERCISE ⋙
A Job Well Done

Select one of the rituals in this chapter. Set a timer for nine minutes.

In your journal, write about your selected ritual as if you have just performed it—and that it went very, very well. Focus on how good the ritual made you feel, from your heart skipping a beat in anticipation to the tingles on your scalp in the presence of a healing power. Include the ways that you always know deep down that the magic is working or the gods are near. If it helps, go through the entire ritual in your mind's eye as you write, remembering that you're describing a rite during which everything goes right.

nine
Prayers, Offerings, Dreams, and Spells

In my research and interviews, I've identified four esoteric areas that may be impacted by, and can impact, the relationship with depression. I have lumped these together loosely into the acronym "PODS," which stands for prayer, offerings, dreams, and spells. These categories are not entirely distinct, nor is each one expressed in the same proportion on every religious path. What's important is to be able to observe how these factors play in one's own life, and how it changes over time, as a way to understand and manage that relationship.

Prayers

Under "prayer" falls a form of communication that is quite controversial in pagan circles. Two powerful Wiccans I have known helped me understand the poles of thinking on the issue. One of my earliest teachers was a Wiccan initiate, and in a letter I confided how uneasy I was with the way a fellow student appeared to put on airs. In the response, I was reminded that pride comes before a fall, and "it is on our knees that we best pray." On the other side is the late Judy Harrow, founder of the Protean tradition, who once in my presence at a conference talked about a particularly difficult situation that seemed like it had no resolution. "In thirty years as a witch, it was the first time I thought to pray," Harrow said at the time. Later Harrow explained to me that this was because of Gardinerian teachers who had impressed the idea that magic is used to change the world and solve problems; praying "feels like begging," which is why Harrow would never have thought of it first.

That idea of "begging" is not entirely wrong. In *How to Heal Yourself When No One Else Can*, Amy B. Scher refers to prayer as "graceful begging."[44] What Harrow saw as prayer's weakness, Scher frames as its strength. Given that depression brings with it feelings of hopelessness and helplessness, I do not personally see a downside to a little begging. It may be for some readers that—like Harrow—prayer is going to be one of the very last tools tried, but that only means it's not the right tool just yet. Be familiar with it, because it may come in handy.

Prayer also has some research backing up its effects, even if scientists haven't exactly quantified *why* it works. Psychiatrist Bick Wanck writes about the work of Dawson Church, who "concluded, 'In order for prayer and intentionality to be powerful, it must be deeply personal and sincerely engaged.' As you might expect, prayer works best when you really mean it."[45]

Neither Harrow nor Scher seem to be referring to the notion of reciting a memorized or written verse. What's inferred is spontaneous, or at least extemporaneous, exposition. Reciting prayers is certainly a form of praying, but not all praying is reciting prayers. Prayers can stack up, can be counted, and have a plural, while praying is an uncountable act that simply lasts until it's done. In Hel-

---

44. Scher, *How to Heal Yourself*, 55-8

45. Wanck, *Mind Easing*, 177.

lenic tradition, prayers—the writing and the reciting of them—can be offerings, and praying might be anything from adoration to supplication. I think both can be handy. I introduced this prayer to do one small thing in the section about food, but I find it helps whenever a task that is sometimes easy feels completely out of reach.

◥§ EXERCISE §◤
Prayer to Do One Small Thing

What you'll do:

1. Identify a task that is sometimes easy to do, but at the moment feels overwhelming.

2. Recite this prayer:
   Shining ones, if you will it,
   may I see past the fog
   to do this small thing.

3. Begin the task right away.

4. If you continue to have difficulty, repeat the prayer as necessary as you work through the task.

5. Sometimes the task is too big at the moment. If you fall short, forgive yourself and schedule a time to try again. Ask for help if needed.

6. When you complete the task, make a record of it in a journal, or confide in a pet, or tell a trusted friend to ensure that you remember this victory.

When you recite the prayer to do one small thing, do the thing right then, or at least try to do the thing immediately. Recite it like a mantra as you work through the task. It's okay if you fall short of doing the thing right now. When you're ready, try again.

I made that prayer short because I wanted it to be easy to copy down and keep in one's wallet, perhaps, or to memorize. Readers who keep something of a regular practice might have longer prayers memorized. I have several that I use in my daily devotions, and if I get that feeling that an invisible fist is suddenly closing around my spirit, I find I can draw strength by reciting a litany of epithets of Poseidon, for example. It matters less what the words mean and more that it evokes your relationship with one or more deities or universal forces. (I try to be inclusive in my language. I am a theist through and through, and I do draw strength from those relationships, but I don't think you need to conceive of discrete and individual gods to achieve the same benefits.)

Here are a couple of hymns I have written to my patron deity, Poseidon, that I sometimes use as prayers during dark times:

Poseidon's Hope
Darkness.
Deeper than the eye can plumb,
yet still rippling, still roiling,
pulsing from ink to pitch and back.
Too deep for words.

Pressure.
Like a fist that can crush an egg
but not a stone,
that can drive air from lungs
and force ideas to flee.

Hope.
In the depths beyond the sun's reach,
In the crucible that reshapes rock,

In places where drowning is unimagined
as air itself is not known,
Life.

Light.
Skotitas rules the depths,
and bids the fish live.
Skotitas rules the depths,
and his subjects bring light.

Light is hope.
Light is a promise.
Praise Poseidon, by whose will
we shall never dwell in darkness.[46]

Prayer for Those Adrift

What brought them to the rolling seas
was violence, force, a striking change.
What made these humans refugees
may feel fantastic, even strange.

Pelagaeus Poseidon
within your grasp they float,
lives reduced to mere detritus
small and helpless, but a mote.

To board a raft, a boat, a ship,
a transaction in the night,
is to throw the dice in desperation,
on one side fright, beside it plight.

---

46. Ward, *Depth of Praise*, 49.

In your hands they place their beings,
though your name's not likely known
or they'd beg for all safe passage
beyond Epaktaios' throne.

On their behalf, I ask safe passage
for those adrift and lost,
the vulnerable, the hungry,
in every way the storm-tossed.

May the blessings of a glass-calm sea
fall upon the drifting masses.
As secure as Asphaleios,
feeling not the briny lashes.

But for those whose fate is not to land
upon a peaceful shore,
and instead will know Skotitas
in the murky depths of yore,

Should Labrandeus decree
that their journey's end is nigh,
and bid Poseidon Psychopompos
guide them where and tell them why,

May their final breath be sweet,
fear and pain evaporate,
and may they have descendants
their names to venerate.[47]

Prayer of the extemporaneous sort is more likely to include the aforementioned "graceful begging." Whether it's pleading or

---

47. Ward, *Depth of Praise*, 53-4.

positioning, confession or catharsis, this is a chance to take some of what's eating at one's insides and pull it out for inspection. Even for an ardent atheist, this has value the same way that keeping a journal might—but without there being a record of those thoughts. This is an opportunity to examine and process emotions that might be blocking healing. Anyone who believes in a compassionate or abundant universe, or who suspects that the universe is making life difficult on purpose, may find that the process of prayer helps put one's feelings about the universe in perspective. It's hard to accept that one is significant enough to be singled out for suffering, yet also insignificant enough never to be cut a single break. The truth is almost always more nuanced than that. If you believe in gods, you have a ready line of communication with those gods through prayer, albeit a one-way line. How we receive messages from the gods can vary, but I find that it's often easier to start a conversation than wait for the other party to be in the mood. Don't be afraid to be the one to make the call. Open your heart and tell them what you need them to hear.

Prayer is challenging to research using the scientific method, but a 2009 study led the authors to conclude, "Direct contact person-to-person prayer may be useful as an adjunct to standard medical care for patients with depression and anxiety."[48] It might be interesting to repeat this study using people who follow religions wherein science is considered a gift from the gods, rather than an affront to them.

---

48. Peter A. Boelens, Roy R. Reeves, William H. Replogle, and Harold G. Koenig, "A Randomized Trial of the Effect of Prayer on Depression and Anxiety." *International Journal of Psychiatry in Medicine* 39, no. 4 (2009): 377-392. https://doi.org/10.2190/pm.39.4.c.

Offerings

These categories are loose and flowing, which is why *prayers* can sometimes be *offerings*. Offerings are another form of communication, but while prayer is usually words, offerings are gestures. Giving someone a gift is a nice gesture. Receiving gifts can feel good, too. Giving freely and without expectation of something in return is a really nice place to be. That isn't to say that wanting something in return is greedy, although expecting something specific in return doesn't mean that this is not a gift. Offerings are a form of reciprocity. This is not a transaction with immediate payment, or terms agreed upon with the help of lawyers. In a healthy reciprocal relationship, gifts are received by all parties. These relationships are not necessarily direct ones either. My mother may give me food, and I give my younger sibling attention. The same is true when the reciprocity is with gods. I know that I have blessings in my life. I also know that I make offerings to certain gods. I thank the gods for my blessings, but I cannot always attribute any particular instance of good fortune to any god at all. I don't make offerings as bribes. If you want to ask for something specific, see "prayer."

◄§ EXERCISE §►
Make a List of Offerings

What you'll need: a writing implement and writing surface.
What you'll do:

1. Take several cleansing breaths.
2. Bring up memories of times you have celebrated gods, spirits, or the wonder of life.
3. Write down as many possible offerings that come to mind, including ones you've made in the past, as well

as ones you've heard others have made and any others that rise in your mind. Do not judge the suggestions, simply jot them down as quickly as you can.

4. Review the list, eliminating offerings you cannot easily obtain.

5. Make a plan to obtain one or more items on your final list to use as offerings in the future.

Dreams

Depending on one's perspective, *dreams* are either mental detritus being cleared away, or communications with the unconscious part of the mind. I do not think either interpretation rules out messages from gods arriving in dreams. However, dreams can be quieted or darkened in depression, making it more challenging to use them as a resource. Instead of fretting over months or years without recalling a single dream, accept that a forgotten dream does no harm. Disturbing dreams can be unsettling. I find myself particularly bothered by being startled awake by my pounding heart, yet unable to recall what had wrenched me from sleep. Recurring dreams are a sign of some unresolved, stressful situation that needs to be addressed. It may be something obvious, like an upcoming test or job performance review, but it could be coming from someplace deeper. Recurring dreams are worth mentioning to a therapist.[49]

I think the presence and quality of recalled dreams is itself a tool. If dreams go away or begin to be more troubling while in depression, then returning or more pleasant dreams might signal an end to that period. If gods are going to use dreams as a vehicle

---

49. Carr, "What's Behind Your Recurring Dreams?"

then they certainly can during depression, but they may choose to avoid it at this time. Some gods become more present to some adherents during depression, but I don't have any information about how they use dreams in those relationships. Dreams might just not be a particularly smooth road through depression, for gods and mortals alike. Keeping a dream journal might be instructive, or at least help put the bad ones out of the mind for now.

◂§ EXERCISE §▸
Keep a Dream Journal

What you'll need:

- a computer file or notebook—this can be an existing journal or something separate, as you wish.
- a writing implement, if you're using paper.

What you'll do:

1. Place your dream journal near your bedside, someplace you're likely to see it immediately upon waking.
2. Schedule a regular bedtime for yourself, and commit to disconnecting from all screens half an hour ahead of that time.
3. When you retire, ask the universe or your gods to send you a dream, and to allow you to recall it.
4. If upon waking you do recall any snippets of a dream, write down as much detail as you can before doing anything else—even going to the bathroom may be enough to forget the experience.
5. If you do not recall any dreams, rest assured that you did dream.
6. Repeat the above steps each night and morning.

There is no requirement to look over your dream journal, but it can be curious reading if you decide to take the plunge. Depending on your point of view, these might be silly nonsense stemming from neurons firing, or they may be messages from a part of yourself or from another being that could be important. I cannot give a definitive answer, but I suspect that all of these are always true in some proportion.

Spells

Spells, like prayer, are not something that resonates with every pagan. When I first discovered that magic and psychic development were a central part of witchcraft, I was actually a bit disappointed, because I wanted to be on a path to discover the gods, and the do-it-yourself model of magic was a little bit terrifying for me. I knew that I wasn't ready to wield such a powerful tool, and steered clear of magic until I had more age and perspective. Like Joshua Tenpenny, I do not see magic as central to my religious practice, but it is an important part of the practice for many others. One advantage of having magic be central to a religious path is that the ethics are built right in as part of that religion. In fact, the main reason I avoided magic when I was younger is because my Wiccan teachers impressed upon me that I was responsible for what I brought into the world.

Spells work during depression, but it can be like flying blind. As both Ivo Dominguez, Jr. and Courtney Weber attest, magic isn't impacted by depression. If someone has the training and has developed the discipline for practicing magic, depression will not take that away because magic isn't based on belief any more than physics is. Just as a blindfolded soldier can field-strip a firearm, a trained practitioner can still cast a spell. Muscle memory might not be the best way to describe it, but the conscious mind does not need to be engaged if other channels run deep enough. This may not be a good time to learn magic, but if you have some mastery it is not going to disappear. "I have had power even when I don't believe in it," said Weber, recalling a time of being talked into working magic to help someone sell a house, but "I wasn't feeling it. I put together a spell involving a candle and some chili peppers just to show support to the person, and the house burned to the ground the next week." It reminded her of her love and awe for magic.

"Depression and magic can coincide," Dominguez said. "I've had my own bouts, as have many; the world is grey, food isn't as good, nothing's as lively." During peak moments of magic, "it's the reverse," with colors seeming brighter and hyper-realistic. There is a "melding a blurring, everything more united, yet sharper in focus." Nevertheless, "In my twenties, I did significant useful magic despite barely being able to drag myself out of bed." This was possible when it was to help another person. He said it "depends on the nature of the person and their temperament. I have a strong sense of duty to others, and regardless of how exhausted, depressed, down in dumps I am, for a real need I can." On the other hand, "For myself, forget about it." Asked to elaborate, Dominguez said, "It's very hard, I find, to do effective magic for oneself if there is no sense of connection to the beauty and power I experience when I do magic." However, working a spell for someone in need can have its own benefits. "There is a short respite afterwards for me," he said, which could be "sense of accomplishment, or maybe a dopamine-serotonin dance, but I get relief from it."

For those of a different temperament or level of training than Dominguez, there can be depression of sensitivity to the flow of energy, there can be a depression of motivation to work magic, and there can be a depression in belief that it's even worth the effort, but that doesn't mean that magic is itself suppressed, according to Dominguez. "If you do the things to focus the mind and move the energy, it will work whether or not you feel it. If you've developed the practice of doing it, it will happen. Musicians can perform beautifully when feeling like crap, and a lack of depression does not make better musicians," nor does confidence alone grant them skill. The idea that depression blocks magic can in part be tied to New Age practices that have entered Paganism. Belief in magic is not necessary; *skill* in magic is necessary. It's not an issue "if you have developed the craft. The part of you that's depressed is not the totality if your self-hood, it's just the waking consciousness. Other parts know how to do magic too."

While Dominguez is clear that belief has nothing to do with how magic works, losing belief in yourself can make it harder to sort laundry, much less work up the motivation to cast a spell. Depression's interference with magic should not come as a surprise. As Orion Foxwood observed, it can arrive at periods of transition, liminal points when barriers are thin. Those are also the best times for magic, according to some practitioners. Kirk White, for example, teaches that lining up liminal aspects can enhance a spell. Performing it at sunrise or sunset on a solstice while standing in a doorway during a new moon, for example. We become susceptible to depression when we exceed our stress threshold—a line that's unfortunately invisible—and working magic contributes to stress as much as any other exertion. It may not be coincidence that magic also can coincide with transitions.

To be clear, the interference is in how well we perceive the work, which isn't the same as hampering our skills. "Even people that do a lot of [magic] tend to forget that most of their capacity is not vested in the small fragment that interacts in mundane life. Our personality [and] sense of self is about as much as the key to the car; we are not the motor. Sometimes just being able to take the key out and turn it takes all that you've got," Dominguez said. However, just because I think I could drive home from the office with my eyes closed doesn't mean I really want to test that idea. Magic works as much as it always has, but it's not a bad idea to proceed with caution for that reason.

Let's consider some spells one might work that target the relationship with depression itself. As readers may recall from part one, depression is shifty and tries to avoid being pinned down by a definition. These spells include assumptions about the nature of depression which are sometimes at odds with one another. Choose only those spells that speak to your own relationship with depression.

☙ EXERCISE ❧
Binding Depression

This spell uses a physical object to represent depression, which will doubtless remind readers of the depression totem. These objects have very different purposes: one is treated like a long-term house guest that you're working with to find a new home, while the other is being tied up and shoved in a box. If you are inclined to create a depression totem, do not also use this spell. If you are inclined to bind your depression, do not create a totem. The approach you take is a personal choice, but you cannot treat any person in both ways and expect it to go well.

What you'll need:

- a piece of brown paper torn—not cut—from a bag or package paper, roughly square and several inches on a side.
- a writing implement.
- an object that reminds you of your experience of depression.

- a cardboard box—with lid or flaps intact—large enough to fit your symbolic object; if there's a lot of extra room, fill it with crumpled paper or some other packing material.
- a ball or spool of black cord or thread.

What you'll do:

1. Write the phrase "the depression" three times across the brown paper, each below the last like a grocery list.

2. Strike out the word "the" in each case, and write the word "my" above it.

3. Turn the paper ninety degrees.

4. Write the word "bound" three times across previous words; the result should look like a grid pattern, and it's okay to stretch the letters out to make that work.

5. Fold the paper in half toward you, turn 90 degrees and fold again, and continue until the paper can no longer be folded in half; set aside.

6. Hold up the symbolic object and say, "I name this object a proxy for my depression, because _____," filling in the reason(s) why you chose this object. Then say, "By my will and according to the free will of all, I shall bind my depression."

7. Place the object in the cardboard box, packing it in if needed, and close the top—it should not rattle in a way that would make anyone curious about the contents.

8. Placing the folded brown paper atop the box, take up the black cord or thread. Beginning at the top, wrap the cord three times around the box, moving away from you over the top and toward you along the bottom. Turn the box to the left 90 degrees and wrap it thrice more.

Continue wrapping three times and turning to the left until the box is tightly tied shut, and then some; during this entire process you may recite the following: "I wrap this box in sets of three, and thus, depression, I bind thee."

9. Tie the cord off at the top.

10. Store the entire mess on a shelf where you will see it regularly, as a reminder that depression is caged.

❧ EXERCISE ☙
A Bath to Break the Curse of Depression

This spell assumes that since depression can feel like a curse, it can be broken like a curse.

What you'll need:

• a bathtub and a way to fill it with water.

• a cup or bowl of salt.

• a clean washcloth.

What you'll do:

1. During the waning moon, draw yourself a bath.

2. Hold up the salt and say: "Spirits of earth and water, you know me, you know my ancestors, you know my gods. In all our names I call upon thee to cleanse me of any and all magic that is now doing me harm, and to restore me to a place of harmony and wellness. By our wills and according to the free will of all, so mote it be."

3. Pour the salt into the tub and stir it widdershins as it dissolves.

4. Enter the tub yourself and relax in the water for no fewer than nine minutes as the saltwater draws out the negative energy.

5. When you're ready to get out, wipe your body with care as you visualize what remains of the curse being wiped back into the water.

6. Thank the elemental spirits, saying: "I thank you, oh spirits of water and earth, and I bless you in the names of my gods and my ancestors. Go now about your business with glad hearts, and may you again willingly heed my call, should I have need."

7. Open the drain and turn your back on the tub as you dry off and dress yourself. Leave the room without turning back, and do not return until the tub is empty.

◄§ EXERCISE §►
Spell to Protect Against Depression

This spell is based on the assumption that depression—or the factors that cause it—come from outside the self and are also malevolent, to some extent. Whether depression is purely an invading spirit or it's just made possible because mean people and tough breaks chip away at our spiritual immunity, this spell may bolster those natural defenses.

What you'll need:

- a piece of tiger's eye.
- frankincense (resin or a piece of an incense stick).
- rosemary.
- thyme.

- a piece of brown paper, roughly square, torn from a paper bag or package paper.
- a pouch that's just about large enough to fit everything above.
- writing implement.

What you'll do:

1. On the paper, write the word "depression" three times, each below the last as if you're making a list.

2. Turn the paper to the right ninety degrees, and now write the word "freedom" three times in the same manner, such that it crosses the previous writing and the words form a grid.

3. Place the herbs and stone upon the paper, and wrap it up by folding it away from yourself, turning it ninety degrees to the right, folding again, and continuing until the bundle it complete.

4. Place the bundle in the pouch, which you'll keep nearby. Slip it into your bag, attach it to your keys, wear it around your neck, or otherwise keep it within reach.

⋅§ EXERCISE ॐ⋅
Sun Box Spell

This spell, created by Silver Ravenwolf, was performed for me by a dear friend who found it in *Llewellyn's 1995 Magical Almanac*. The box was given to me on the winter solstice, after several of us charged it with the energy of the sun. The purpose is to "uplift the spirits and chase away the blues"[50] and should be done on a

---

50. Silver Ravenwolf, *Llewellyn 1995 Magical Almanac*, (St. Paul, MN: Llewellyn Publications, 1994), 259–60.

Sunday, when the moon is in Leo, or empower when the planetary hour is in the sun.

What you'll need:

- one small, wooden box.
- blue acrylic paint.
- yellow acrylic paint.
- white or silver acrylic paint.
- flat brush for blue paint.
- round brush for white or silver paint.
- gold sequins.
- craft glue.
- one small gold candle that will fit inside the box.

What you'll do:

1. Cleanse and consecrate all materials.
2. Paint the box blue on the outside. Allow it to dry.
3. Paint small stars in white/silver on the outside of the box. Allow it to dry.
4. Paint the inside of box yellow. Allow it to dry.
5. Open the box, brush inside the bottom with glue. Sprinkle sequins over the glue, and cover entire surface. Let it dry.
6. Repeat the procedure with the inside top of box and the inside sides.
7. When the timing is right, empower the box with love, divine energy, success, and wisdom.
8. Dress the gold candle with an oil that is pleasing to your purpose. Put it in the box.

9. Close the box. Do not open it again. Seal the box with a bit of wax.

10. Design a card explaining the purpose of the box. On a day when your friend is feeling blue, they are to open the box, relax, and burn the candle.

⚜ EXERCISE ⚜
Depression Mirror Spell

What you'll need:

- a small mirror; either a hand mirror or standing mirror works.
- a soft cloth, suitable for cleaning the mirror.
- candle (optional).
- incense (optional).
- Either Florida water, khernips, or another purifying liquid.

What you'll do:

1. Set up the mirror on a desk, shelf, or table that you can look at without craning your neck.

2. Lower the light level in the room.

3. If you like, enhance your focus with the use of a candle or incense.

4. If you like, use the Florida water or other liquid to purify yourself before you settle in.

5. Take up a comfortable position before the mirror. You may close your eyes, or look with open eyes into the middle distance in the direction of the mirror, not focusing on any particular details in your reflection.

6. Allow your thoughts to drift, acknowledging each that arises and then releasing it.

7. Say, "I see you."

8. Focus on your reflection. See your face. See the eyes, windows to the soul, and acknowledge their depth. If you experience negative feelings about yourself in this moment, acknowledge them, but instead of dwelling on them breathe on the mirror to fog it. If no negative feelings rise, wait for a period of roughly thirty heartbeats before fogging the mirror.

9. Say, "They see me."

10. Either close your eyes or relax your gaze to look toward the mirror without focusing on anything in particular. As the fogged mirror distorts and obscures the reflection, how we see ourselves is not always how others see us. Our pain may be invisible to them, or our flaws much less pronounced.

11. Wipe the mirror clean with the cloth, saying, "I see the good in me that others see." Continue to wipe the mirror and repeat the phrase until the sound of words begins to lose meaning, then stop and fall again into quiet for a time.

12. Place the mirror somewhere you will see it during the day, and pick it up to look at your own reflection when you are struggling. Fog the mirror with your breath if looking at the reflection is difficult, and wipe again as above to strengthen the charge.

It is done.

❦ EXERCISE ❧
A Grooming Mirror Spell

Much of what makes depression challenging is the fact that it whispers in a soft voice that sounds much like your own, a voice that is laden with self-critical talk. It is a voice that has access to the doubts we already hold dear: the sound of your laugh is unpleasant, your weight is too high, others are only pretending to like you, you are socially awkward, no one cares what you think, you should just stay home, you're too lazy to do that, this will fail like all of your ideas fail. Listen to that voice long enough and you will feel uglier, stupider, less loved, and unwelcome. This spell uses literal sight to counter figurative hearing, and a mirror to bounce back that negative self-talk. Perform this spell in a bathroom or wherever you normally would undertake washing and grooming.

What you'll need:

- any mirror that is useful for personal grooming.
- grooming items, such as a toothbrush and toothpaste or powder; razor and shaving cream or soap; facial scrub or cleanser; tweezers; cotton swabs; cosmetics.

What you'll do:

1. Lay your grooming materials out as you would if you were planning on going out someplace dressy, whatever that means to you.

2. Settle into quiet for a time, acknowledging thoughts that arise without fixating on them. Keep your eyes closed or look with open eyes into the middle distance in the direction of the mirror, not focusing on any particular details in your reflection.

3. Say, "You are beautiful, for all that you hide it."

4. Focus on your reflection. See your face, including whatever you consider flaws as well as features you believe are strengths. If you experience negative feelings about yourself in this moment, acknowledge and then release them.

5. Say, "Let us reveal that beauty."

6. Begin breathing in a measured pace: a slow count of four, hold it for four beats, exhale for four beats, and rest for another four. The count is just to slow the breathing down; don't feel you must count aloud. Feel yourself slip into a rhythm of slow, deliberate breathing.

7. Begin as thorough a grooming routine as you can muster. This may include a shower or bath, but must include actions before the mirror such as brushing of teeth, washing the face, exfoliating, or shaving. If personal grooming is something you have avoided recently, make a list if necessary to ensure that you take care of all the necessities as part of this working. Hold in your mind the intention to reveal the beauty of your spirit.

8. If you like, recite lines such as these as you groom:

   - While washing the face: "Let my tears be washed away and my furrowed brow relax."

   - While brushing the hair: "Let my hair shine with love."

   - While shaving: "Let my hidden strength come forth."

   - While applying cosmetics: "Let me wear my shining spirit on the outside."

9. When you have completed all your grooming tasks, either close your eyes or relax your gaze as you look toward the mirror without focusing on anything in particular.

10. Visualize the face of your higher self, your agathos daimon, your guardian spirit, or whatever represents the ideal you in the mirror beside your own

11. In your mind's eye, will your faces to overlap and finally merge.

It is done.

Runes and Sigils

Written symbols, including the letters of runic alphabets as well as sigils, can hold a great deal of power. Runes, such as those found in the futharks and in the ogham script, have been a source of wisdom and esoteric power of centuries. Sigils, which may incorporate runes and English letters, are created to tailor magic more narrowly.

Kari Tauring suggested how several runes that might be useful in managing depression:

- **Nied**, or nauthiz, is called the "need fire." Tauring instructed, "Make a list of your needs. Now make one of your wants. Do they match? Only after meeting our needs can our wants be considered. When relationships are out of balance there is need. Need constricts us so that our actions have deep meaning and purpose. Focus on your wants first and you will always have need. A reversal indicates you are confusing wants and needs."

- **Gifu** (also gebo, or gift) is two straight lines of equal length, leaning into each other and bound at the middle.

Gifting creates relationships. "Remember, you are not alone. Even acknowledgement of the other is a gift. Giving and receiving must be in balance. Imbalance in gifu is actually the rune nied (need). Evaluate all of your relationships to make sure there is equality."

- **Mannaz**, also called man or manaheim, represents human home or community. "This is gifu with legs, the gift rune of relationships held up for all to see. Does your community support your highest good or does it drag you down? If it is good for you, ask it for help and give help in return. A reversal means you should look for a more supportive community."

We will explore the power of community in the next chapter of this book.

One thing I have personally struggled with during periods of depression is out-of-control, ruminative thinking, that runaway thought train that locks me into one emotional track, or derails some emotions entirely to avoid experiencing them.[51] The sigil above can help with that. When thoughts and feelings are piling up and are starting to feel overwhelming, inhale to a slow count of four, and exhale just as slowly while looking at or drawing this sigil to release the need to think about everything *now*. Some thoughts are just going to have to wait. Draw it on the back of your therapist's business card to keep on hand in your wallet or purse. Trace

---

51. Pollan, *How to Change Your Mind*, 379.

it in the condensation of a bathroom mirror, or exhale on a window to make a drawing surface for it.

The design is a simple one because ease of drawing it was a priority. A lot of sigils are quite complex, and the last thing someone experiencing runaway negative or worrying thoughts needs is to fret over whether all the serifs are placed perfectly. It's the breath that charges the sigil, and each copy of this sigil is connected to all others, meaning that every time *anyone* exhales to charge it, *all* copies of it get the boost.

When drawn on paper or any moveable surface, this sigil can be oriented to further shift the consciousness of the user. With the curved side down, it represents the unsteady state of a mind that is burdened by too many thoughts. Rotate it 180 degrees—or simply move to its other side to view it from the opposite direction—and it becomes one of the most stable structures, an arch. For an additional boost, try taking a few moments to ground and center yourself with the sigil in the first position, and then after rotating it take at least five minutes to meditate and clear the mind of thoughts altogether. Even after grounding, meditation can be tricky, as thoughts invariably slip back in. Be patient. Once you recognize a thought, acknowledge it, and then release it rather than dwelling on it. I have had success by simply telling myself "Wait," which reminds me that this is not the time to chase that thought.

Another way to use this sigil is to scratch or carve it into a candle, again breathing on it to charge. The sigil's energy is released by the flame, therefore it should be inscribed someplace that it will be consumed. This is why I prefer a taper candle, as thicker ones are often made with wicks too thin to entirely burn the wax. A column candle can be used, but make sure to inscribe it on the top to ensure that the sigil is completely destroyed. Pick a blue candle to represent emotions or the subconscious. Some might be drawn to black since many of us connect this with the feelings of depression. Black wax is never truly black; it's an extremely dark hue of another color, such as green or blue. Scratch a bit off under a fingernail and have a closer look to see what makes up the black, and select one that is based on blue. The candle can be used in conjunction with meditation, or while making offerings or praying before a depression shrine. Leaving a burning candle unattended is usually a bad idea.

◄§ EXERCISE §►
A Bathing Spell for Easing Depression

Water is the element of emotion; it is seen in the cleansing power of tears, and "drowning" is a word that some would use to describe their experience with depression. I have never figured out how to use a bath to wash my body, but I find it's a powerful way to infuse myself with magical energy by essentially turning me into the main ingredient of a potion. Rest assured, this is not a potion anyone is expected to drink.

What you'll need:

- a bathtub and water with which to fill it.
- a drawstring bag that can get wet, such as one made from muslin cotton or burlap; these can be obtained at craft stores or put together by someone with scraps of fabric and basic sewing skills.
- soaking stones—obtain at least three of the following types of crystals, all of which can be safely submerged:
  - citrine
  - smoky quartz
  - rose quartz

- amethyst
- lapis lazuli
- amber (particularly good if seasonal affective disorder is present)
- aventurine
- ocean jasper
- tiger's eye (particularly good if bipolar disorder is present)
- garnet

- salt (sea salt or kosher salt is preferable, but any salt will do in a pinch, as it were).
- a candle charged for healing (optional).
- herbs to ease depression such as scullcap, vervain, chamomile, lemon balm, passion flower, lemongrass, and peppermint (optional).
- blue thread or embroidery floss.

What you'll do:

To prepare the stones you'll be using:

1. Place the selection of stones in the bag and exhale into it, saying:

    Awaken, o stones, and awaken my true feelings within me.

2. Tie or sew the bag shut with the blue thread or embroidery floss. After you've completed that preparation, the bath itself is prepared the same way each time.

To prepare the bath:

1. If you are using a candle, light it before you start filling the tub. Focus on the flame for a few minutes to help clear your mind.

2. You may get into the tub before or after adding water, as is your usual practice, but do not add the bag of stones until it's at least halfway full of water.

3. Follow this by adding three measures of salt to the water, which will both amplify this healing work and cleanse the stones to use again.

If you're using herbs, sprinkle them over the water as the tub is being filled. Plant matter can clog drains, so use any herbs sparingly!

1. Make the water as hot as is comfortable, which is a personal preference, and sit in the tub as long as your tolerance allows.

2. Allow your mind to drift and do not shy away from strong emotions as they arise. You are in a safe space—a sacred space—and these are emotions which you may need to process to move past the pain that invites depression to be your companion.

3. Once your body becomes uncomfortable due to water temperature or any other reason, open the drain and let the water out, releasing with it those emotions and memories which you experienced.

4. Extinguish the candle, if you used one, and retrieve the bag of stones. Rinse the bag of stones in cold water and set it on a towel or someplace where it can dry in the air. Once it's dry, it can be used again.

It is done.

Candle Magic

Candles are an excellent tool in the management of depression. For one thing, a candle flame is a natural focal point and can make meditation easier. Any candle will do, but if you select one that has been blessed or magically charged, be aware of the intention put into it first. If it's not juiced up to ground or clear the mind, then the candle's purpose might prove to be distracting. A candle charged for a different purpose may make meditation more difficult.

Find a place you can sit down comfortably with the candle before you. Light the candle and look in the direction of the flame without specifically focusing on it. Allow your eyes to relax; this is sometimes described as looking into the middle distance or gazing at the flame with a soft focus. Take in a breath by lowering your diaphragm—pushing out your abdomen—until resistance is felt, pause for a beat, then exhale. Release the breath first by allowing it to come out by pressure alone, then give it a gentle push. As you continue to breathe, let your body's systems take over and do it at a natural pace. If you find yourself focusing on your breath, silently acknowledge the thought and then release it with the next exhalation. Do the same if you find yourself thinking about the flame. Any thought that rises, name and then release it with the outward breath. The goal is to become unaware of any thoughts, but there is no timeline to achieve that. Thoughts will come, be acknowledged, and be released.

⋙ EXERCISE ⋘
Draw Off a Negative Mood with a Candle

What you'll need:

- a black or a white taper candle, picking the one that first comes to mind (*no* second-guessing or overthinking allowed; if necessary, ask a friend, "black or white?" without context and use that response).

What you'll do:

1. Remove any packaging and hold the candle before you, keeping the intention of using it to draw off negative energy and emotion in mind.

2. Take a bit of your own saliva onto your fingers and grasp the candle in the middle of its length.

3. Wipe from the middle down to the bottom, and then from the middle up to the tip (you can also go in both directions at once if you use two hands) to charge it with your intention.

4. Light and sit with the candle for a few minutes when you feel you need it, or anytime you think that lighting a candle couldn't possibly help.

5. To ensure you will use it, keep the candle someplace you'll see it, or set some kind of reminder to check in and use it; you may wish to make use of this candle as part of a regular meditation practice.

⋅§ EXERCISE ⋟⋅
Candle Spell to Find a Therapist

There are many potential barriers to finding a therapist, starting with the idea that one needs a therapist in the first place. The benefits of therapy are explored more thoroughly in the "community" section, but here is a spell to help someone who is ready for therapy to find a professional who is a good fit. Kelden Mercury provided the initial inspiration for this simple spell, which can be expanded by incorporating crystals, herbs, planets, and other forces that correspond to the goal.

What you'll need:

- a blue candle.
- matches or a lighter.
- a piece of brown paper, roughly square, torn from a paper bag or package paper (optional).
- a writing implement (optional).
- inscribing tool (optional).
- journal (optional).

What you'll do:

1. The candle is blue to promote communication. Using the inscribing tool or a fingernail, carve into the wax words or symbols that you desire in a therapist, such as respect, open-mindedness, or accessibility.

2. On the paper, expand on what you've carved to provide clarity if needed. If you do this, place the paper underneath the candle.

3. Lick your thumb and rub it over the carvings to seal the candle.

4. Light the candle and visualize meeting with a therapist for the first time, discussing issues such as the relationship between your religion and your mental health, and the feeling of "clicking" with this person.

5. When you meet with a potential therapist, endeavor to observe all that is said and done with your whole self: the words, the tone of voice, the smell of the office if you meet in person, the tension in your body, the body language of the therapist, and any cues you can pick up with more subtle senses.

6. After that first meeting, you may wish to enter the impressions from your stream of consciousness into a journal to help you assess the potential of this relationship. If you do this at all, do it as soon as possible after the first session so that it is fresh in your mind.

◄§ EXERCISE §►
Assessing PODS in Your Life

A PODS assessment is to take stock of how prayer, offerings, dreams, and spells are represented in one's life right now.

Using the below scale, how important are each of the following aspects in my life today?

1-very unimportant

2-somewhat unimportant

3-neither important nor unimportant

4-somewhat important

5-very important

- Prayer
- Offerings
- Dreams
- Spells

Using the below scale, how recently have I experienced each of the following?

1-longer than a month ago

2-in the past month

3-in the past week

4-in the past day

5-several times in the past day

- Prayer
- Offerings
- Dreams
- Spells

As a snapshot, these answers might not be especially useful, but try taking this quick self-assessment daily or weekly and then plot it out on a graph. If you are also tracking your mood, you might see even more patterns emerge. Do you find you dream more or less during depression? Are offerings and gods more prominent, or is that altar collecting more dust than usual? When are you led to pray? These data can help you understand the ebb and flow of your relationship with depression, and perhaps what triggers flare-ups for you. As with all ideas presented in this book, readers are invited to explore at their own pace rather than trying to do all the things at once.

⁕ JOURNAL EXERCISE ⁂
Spice and Everything Nice

Bring your journal with you into the kitchen, pantry, or wherever herbs and spices are kept in your home. Line up as many spice bottles or containers of fresh herbs as you like along the counter. One by one, open the container, smell the herb or spice, and write down the first thing that comes to mind: a memory, a feeling, a meal, or whatever thought the plant triggered.

Circle the ones that bring up something positive. Consider using these in your cooking to reinforce those associations.

ten
Community

Isolation is not a healthy human state. We all seek solitude from time to time, but isolation is imposed, rather than sought. That's because community dilutes depression, making it the one thing we are likely to avoid. Depression is a spirit that prefers a human host, and modifies the behavior of that host to make it a more comfortable home for depression. For that reason, we can observe the behavior of people experiencing depression to infer the conditions that make the human a welcoming home. These include unpleasant mood swings that wear thin on others, avoidance of other people including friends and loved ones, and reduced interest in going out or cultivating a welcoming home. If this is the case, then it appears depression is steering its hosts away from social connection and community, instilling a sense of anxiety and revulsion to keep us from sharing love and camaraderie with others of our own kind.

Recurrence of depression is not guaranteed, but the odds are high. 50 percent of people who have one episode of depression have another one, and 80 percent of those who have that second episode will have a third.[52] There are several factors that appear

---

52. Bursuca, Stephanie L. and William G. Iacono. "Risk for Recurrence in Depression." Clinical Psychology Review 27, no. 8 (December 2007): 959-985. https://doi.org/10.1016/j.cpr.2007.02.005.

to be indicators of how likely someone is to have a recurrence of depression, one of which is how strong a social support system one has. Another term for this might be "community." While that word is sometimes used to refer to a named geographic area, the true value of community is engaging with neighbors and developing friendships. Pagans, being members of a rather small slice of modern society that is itself sliced into groups with widely different belief systems, are often more mindful of the value of community because of how hard it can be to connect with others who share those beliefs, practices, or values. Pagan versions of community might be built around one or more events held throughout the year, online connections, or be organized around very small groups for practice. Community thrives best when members spend regular time together physically, which was a challenge long before the pandemic of the 2020s caused people the world over to rethink travel plans. There is also value in diversity, and building community among one's neighbors is important even if none of them share the same religious outlook, because being physically present appears to have benefits that a purely distant relationship may not. Many do not find what they seek from a purely online community, or from a community with a very small number of people, or from one that depends on gathering in person only very infrequently, such as at festivals. That's not to say that community does not thrive despite all of these challenges, but it does mean that our efforts to succeed require a lot of effort.

Courtney Weber resists naming or even acknowledging depression. "'I'm fine' is my usual," Weber said, because she dwells on all the ways in which her life isn't hard and the suffering she is not experiencing and it feels petty to name it. If an experienced witch who has weathered depression for all of her adult life struggles with naming this source of pain, then it's not a weakness any more than vomiting after drinking syrup of ipecac is a weakness. Depression is designed not to be noticed even when it should be impossible to miss.

In the United States, the cultural hallmark of rugged individualism reinforces the wrongheaded idea that we should be able to "walk it off." That's also the advice that used to be given to football players after they sustained traumatic brain injuries. It's not effective in either case. Pulling oneself up by one's bootstraps out of a pit of depression is inordinately difficult, and I submit that it's only ever possible if some deity comes along and offers you a hand. The persistent narrative that people with depression can simply choose to end their own suffering has no basis in real-life experience. For chronic depression, the best balm comes from the community. Here, community can mean anything from family and friends to mental health professionals, spirits, and gods. We are never truly alone, no matter how much the voice of depression whispering in our ear says otherwise.

"Depression is an epidemic," said Weber. "I don't know anyone who isn't; I'm not sure if it's the disconnect from nature, or because we are stripped from community-mindedness. We are not cougars, we are not solo creatures. We're wolves. We're pack animals."

Community: it's often the last thing that someone with depression wants, yet it's a very important part of the healing which is necessary. Maybe many hands make light work of depression, or many shoulders can bear the burdens of one heart, but community is a theme that comes up with good reason. My own hypothesis is that depression turns intuition on its head. Someone in tune with one's own body knows the best things to eat and do for wellness, just based on the nonverbal messages being sent. Depression seems to commandeer that intuition the way a virus takes over cells; instead of this intuitive sense leading the individual toward healing, under depression we instead avoid anything that might weaken depression's hold. Do not interact with other people. Do not prepare healthy meals. Do not exercise. Do not clean yourself or your environment. These habits create a comfortable nest for depression to settle in, rather than a path to wellness and balance. Isolation, processed foods, cobwebs physical and emotional: these are the ingredients for a warm, dark lifestyle in which little energy is devoted to personal care and improvement, and yet it's a lifestyle that leaves those familiar with it feeling completely drained of energy. Where's that energy going?

Isolation is sustenance to one's depression, because there is nothing to redirect energy away from feeding it. "Social distancing" as a mitigation to the pandemic compounds this. Technology is a poor substitute for being physically around people, because we can feel isolated despite it.[53] Humans are social animals, and we must make choices that lean into that reality in order to be hale and well. Concepts like tribalism and nationalism are denounced for some very good reasons, but they are expressions of that deep need to be with one another. At its worst, nationalism is an excuse to treat strangers as criminals, but the ancient Hellenes taught that strangers might just as easily prove to be friends. Gods have long disguised themselves as strangers in need of aid to see what would happen, and those myths may also be an expression of our need to be with one another. Unfortunately, the fear, mistrust, and outright hatred seems to have eclipsed our desire to take care of one's own, throwing the system out of balance; we find it more difficult to understand what it is to be a neighbor or a friend. Depression

---

53. Harris, Rebecca. "The Loneliness Epidemic," The Independent, March 30, 2015. https://www.independent.co.uk/life-style/health-and-families/features/loneliness-epidemic-more-connected-ever-feeling-more-alone-10143206.html.

does not create the many factors that drive us into isolation, but it thrives in that condition.

Community is the cure for isolation. I would not go so far as to say that community cures depression, but it does appear clear that replacing isolation with interaction should inhibit its growth. This is a spirit that thrives in secrecy and darkness. Depression has a much harder time growing when one is surrounded by people who know one's moods and attitudes. It's just like how mold rarely grows in a sunlit area, and sexual assault is less likely to occur when there are witnesses around.

Living in close community makes it easier to name depression. One may not recognize it in oneself, but neighbors who see one another often will know that something has changed. "When you're depressed, your instinct is not to get into close community," said Tauring. "It doesn't feel safe." That's one reason why getting into closer community is important for health. "Being around the same group of people once or twice a week" is what's needed. Typical coworkers in a capitalist job—people we only see at work and have little interest in talking to otherwise—may not fit the bill for many of us, since we are often guarded in that environment.

Given that depression feeds off and amplifies feelings of inadequacy, it should be understandable how important the company of other humans is to addressing depression. Humans are social beings, and we socialize best with other humans. Moreover, there is evidence that social interaction actually bolsters the immune system.[54] Solitude can be a choice and it is healthy to seek it out with intention, but being forced into it out of an inability to interact

---

54. Holt-Lunstad, Julianne. "Besides Feelings Of Loneliness, What Else Does Isolation Do To Us?" Interview by Steve Inskeep. Morning Edition, NPR, June 16, 2020. Audio, 6:59. https://www.npr.org/2020/06/16/877778770/besides-feelings-of-loneliness-what-else-does-isolation-do-to-us.

is not the same thing as a choice. It is worthwhile to put intention into choosing relationships as well. If you do not articulate and focus your intention, depression can and will help you select people who will feed and amplify the depression. On the other hand, pruning the unhealthy relationships and nurturing the positive ones will aid in healing faster and more completely than any other form of relationship can. Community is the most powerful magic available to humans, and its power is working all the time. It's unfortunate that this power is frequently unfocused, which may be why so many things can feel like they are going awry.

Community dilutes depression, and not just because it will not be affecting all of us in the same way at the same time. I write this at a time when reported periods of depression are skyrocketing, largely because of the imposed isolation of the pandemic. It is the connections between people—the ones always eroded by depression, the ones that when eroded by external factors can make it easier for depression to settle in—that make this spirit wither or withdraw. To be clear, while social interactions are demonstrably part of depression management, I am going beyond what is known through science when I say that community is the key to a solution. There is more to human connection than we yet have proven to be true, but we continue to learn more about the benefits of social contact, as well as the best ways to foster it. We do not practice community in a way that it is a panacea for depression, but I'm clear that there is an untapped power there worth understanding.

Writing, for all that it has helped this author put food on the table, is really low down on the hierarchy of methods to connect with other humans. That's especially true in the internet age, when it's possible to fire off a text or an email quickly and get a response sometimes just moments later. Writing is removed from all social cues that signal intent and mood, and our brains fill in those pieces based on our own mood and past history. In other words, a written electronic conversation is more a conversation with oneself than with the other person. Writing is also the go-to method when there is reason to believe that it may get awkward, such as after a long absence or when emotions have been running high. However, there is research supporting the idea that talking is superior when connection is the goal instead of conveying information.[55] I have certainly gone the writing route myself, but that study makes me realize that it can be better to get over my distaste for phone conversation. It's superior to writing, but still falls short of being physically present, something that is frustratingly curtailed in a time of pandemic.

How, then, do we manage during periods when isolation is imposed by fiat, or becomes the norm because there's no place where people can gather? I write this as humans are avoiding one another to prevent transmission of a coronavirus, but I expect we may face similar challenges in the future. Taking pains to practice good hygiene and gathering only in very small groups appears to be sufficient to minimize the spread of this particular virus, and those strictures don't have to mean dismantling the concept of community. We don't get the benefits of community when we attend a massive concert or athletic event, or by visiting a large amusement park. Community is about connecting at a block party or around a fire, sitting for the neighbors' children and borrowing their tools, getting to know individuals in a way that just isn't possible via the internet alone. It's the normalization of other people, allowing them to make the transition from a bunch of facts (vegan, brown hair, rides a bicycle) into a familiar person who is expected

55. Reynolds, Emily. "Phone Calls Help Create Closer Bonds Than Texting." Research Digest, October 8, 2020. https://digest.bps.org.uk/2020/10/08/phone-calls-help-create-closer-bonds-than-texting/.

to have complex views and emotions and actions that may be confusing or contradictory as well as delightful and annoying, for that's the full human experience. It's being able to disagree on some things—even many—but still feel a level of caring by one for the other.

Tauring speaks of the Finnish approach, in which one is open about the experience of depression and in turn receives companionship and support. It is much, much harder to engage in the habits that arise from depression—such as alterations to sleep schedule and diet—if one remains engaged in community. Social accountability can keep depression from turning into long periods without bathing or long periods without leaving home. Social peers may be more likely than coworkers to note when your temper seems out of scale or your tone overly critical—or they might be, if they are aware that you have entered a period of depression. Left unchecked, these changes can easily lead to missed days of work or conflict on the job, with unemployment being a very real outcome of depression. As it happens, in a 2013 Gallup survey, more than twice the unemployed respondents reported feelings of depression than the employed ones.[56] This fits a perverse pattern that often rises with depression: the things that happen because one is in depression are often themselves factors that now contribute to keeping one in depression. This is the dark cone of power that depression raises from the essence of its host. In this case, it can lead not only to questioning one's self-worth, but also to isolation. It's no wonder that depression rates

---

56. Adams, Susan. "How Unemployment And Depression Fit Together." Forbes, June 9, 2014. https://www.forbes.com/sites/susanadams/2014/06/09/how-unemployment-and-depression-fit-together/.

have tripled in the United States during the 2020 coronavirus pandemic, which attacks social connection in a very direct manner.[57]

Community is not helpful for Sarah W. for reasons that are all too familiar. "Online isn't useful to me, and I don't have local community. It's a private, personal struggle for me, but I think there might be benefits [to community] if in person." Sarah W. is not alone in lacking in-person connection to others of like mind. Our interview took place before the term "social distance" moved in to stay, and it's now abundantly clear that while communicating through devices is better than complete isolation, community has a physical aspect that feeds the spirit. As discussed in the section on strategies for spirit, community can include many types of beings, in addition to the human ones. However, depression eats at the connecting tissue of relationships, and when a being has no physical presence this might be an easier connection to attack. Relationships with animal companions are on the other end of that spectrum in many cases, and I've had people tell me that the need to care for a pet is sometimes all that gets them out of bed on a bad day. Physical connection is important, and a virus that blocks that connection is downright insidious.

As opposed to Sarah W., Joshua Tenpenny is in a pagan group largely to belong to a community. "I like the fellowship, but I don't like doing rituals together; not like I dislike them, but they don't connect for me like individual experiences." I had a similar relationship with football. I do not care for the sport, but I used to join friends who were fans of the local team every week during the season. The game didn't do anything for me, but being surrounded by

---

57. Berman, Robby. "US Cases of Depression Have Tripled During the COVID-19 Pandemic." *Medical News Today*, September 19, 2020. https://www.medicalnewstoday.com/articles/us-cases-of-depression-have-tripled-during-the-covid-19-pandemic.

friends on an emotional roller coaster was a magical experience. The reason I set aside my Sunday afternoons had little to do with football and everything to do with community.

❧ EXERCISE ☙
Put Yourself Out There

Think about an activity that a group of your friends or coworkers do together that you have avoided because it's boring, or stupid, or it's too noisy there, or you feel self-conscious, or you need to feed your cat at that time. Take a mental step back to see that the activity is not the reason they gather, but just an excuse. Adults find it difficult just to knock on someone's door to see if they want to come out and play. Your inner child understands that the point is not winning the game or consuming beverages or shuffling cards, but being with other people. Give yourself permission to take part next time you're invited, or even to ask to be included. Even if you're not comfortable throwing yourself into the activity or the conversation, be open to basking in the glow of community when you do.

Therapy

In a certain sense, therapy and community provide the same thing: support and context for processing emotions. Ideally, one will have access to both of these, but the nature of depression tends to erode access to either. Hopefully the reader has access to at least one of the two. Therapy is not a replacement for loving supportive relationships, nor can members of your wider community be expected to be able to provide the focused help a trained therapist can offer. That's not to say that one cannot overcome depression without both, but it's one more factor that can make an uphill climb more difficult to complete. Spirits and gods and trees and animals also have a part to play in this supportive net. No one should practice anything as dangerous as living without a net. Nets are there to keep us from falling to our doom. Weave your own net out of the fibers you have available, and tend to it! Replace weakening cords, tighten knots, and be on the lookout for new pieces to include. That could be a new friend or social group, a novel form of devotion, a paid talking partner who could be someone as informal as a hairdresser or as structured as a licensed therapist, or caring for a pet. Any nurturing relationship is a net positive for your emotional safety net. While writing this book, I began tending to a wounded tree on my property, and I consider that relationship part of my net. If confiding in your sourdough starter (which benefits from your exhalations because you're providing more yeast) is part of your net, I won't judge.

There are times when it makes sense to talk with someone who is trained to listen and provide support. That way does carry risks, and during a period of depression it's easy to get fixated on what might go wrong. Therapy works when we are able to form a trusting relationship with a stranger. It can take time to build that rapport, and if the relationship sours then that can be discouraging. In this way relationships with therapists are similar to all human relationships; we aren't going to see eye to eye with some people. The healing power of community is much too valuable to discard because individual relationships didn't work out. The way of the hermit might seem appealing, but humans are social animals. Just one bad moment with a therapist is all the spirit of depression needs to try to dissuade you from ever trying again, but if you didn't like what that therapist said to you, why would you readily listen to a spirit that's saying things that are far worse?

Feeling like professionals are phoning it in can be especially hard when experiencing depression. As I said, trust is important when working with a therapist, and when one does not feel heard, one is far less likely to trust. Depression is also characterized by negative self-talk, and when there is an opportunity for trust to erode, that's an opportunity depression will take to discourage further attempts with a professional. It can be very hard to let down emotional walls enough to allow a therapist to gain insight into one's inner workings. The last time I gave it a shot was with a therapist I had already worked with, respected, and trusted. I'd paid top dollar during my first course of treatment, but by the time I returned he was accepting my family's insurance—which, in terms of modern health care, meant less of a profit. During our sessions this therapist was focused on getting me to use a particular form of biofeedback which, it was not lost on me, allowed the doctor to be out of the room for most of the hour. I didn't end the relationship, though, until one of our talk therapy sessions was continually interrupted to work out some logistics for the Beltane festival on that land. I understood that I wasn't the priority, but I didn't take it personally. I did, however, take myself elsewhere.

It is important to remember that mental health counselors and therapists are also human beings, and all human beings have bad days and hidden biases. At the same time, it's the fact that they are human that makes them valuable as therapists in the first place. If you are disappointed by a less-than-ideal first meeting with a therapist, it's okay not to make a second appointment with that individual, but you should instead commit to making an appointment with someone else. My experience is that one is much more likely to have a lackluster experience with a new therapist than a traumatic one, and that the potential benefits outstrip the risks. The process of just deciding to find a therapist can feel exhausting, but the reasons you are seeking help don't just vanish because you had a bad first session. The pitfalls are part of the process.

Raven Kaldera provided some insight into why it can be a monumental task even to look for a therapist: "Depression, like all mental illness, is stigmatized. Any word used to describe a stigmatized identity will eventually become stigmatized itself. Before it was widely understood as a mental illness, having 'the blues' was less stigmatized, but of course nobody could get any help for it. Now it's better understood, at least some people can be helped, but it's irrevocably linked to 'crazy.' People have a hard time acknowledging it. In addition, the nature of chemical depression—which lowers motivation and sabotages the desire to take action—means that doing anything challenging (like getting help) can look like a huge, impossible mountain to climb. This can discourage sufferers from acknowledging the depth of what is wrong."

There are lots of reasons people do not seek treatment when they are struggling, according to Rachel, such as feeling worthless and guilty, and the belief that they should be able to "beat this themselves." Others include worries that talking to a therapist would result in hospitalization against their will, or being forced to take medication when they have an objection to chemicals. Often clients are so tired they can't even consider making a phone call, or they can't decide if it's serious enough. Plus, if you feel like death is the only good solution, you can't imagine anyone could tell you anything different.

Anthony Rella acknowledges that a number of factors can be a barrier to obtaining therapy, the first of which is identifying the need. "It is rather subjective as to whether therapy is needed, and often people wait a long time and would benefit when things are milder. ... You could start by talking to your primary care provider, if you have one, who may have assessment tools available or be able to give some insight into the severity of your symptoms." That said, part of the resistance can arise from a perception of stigma. "People still feel stigma around whether to go to therapy, and in some cases [that stigma]'s really unhelpful. If you're struggling and feeling stuck with your mood, self-esteem, or life satisfaction, you might benefit from having a therapist to talk to. If you even wonder if maybe you should go to therapy, and you have the resources, you might as well go to therapy."

"I don't make the decision to tell a person that they need to see a mental health professional on my own personal judgment," said Kaldera. "I kind of feel like you have to be a mental health professional yourself to say that to a client and have them take it seriously. My clinical judgment is not adequate to make a diagnosis; I don't have the training. On the other hand, I've been a practicing shaman for over twenty years, and so I divine on the matter and tell the person what the gods/spirits say about it. That includes asking them if I should tell this person at all—some may resist the information—and stepping back if the answer is a strong 'no.'"

When I most needed therapy, I was not a willing participant. The reason why it was effective is because I was locked in a mental health ward and had nowhere else to go. Outside of that extreme circumstance, an uncooperative patient will get nothing from therapy, and locking someone inside with a therapist is no guarantee. No matter how dehydrated we become, we will not drink water that is offered until we admit that we are thirsty in the first place.

Whether it's worries over stigma, money, or cultural values, it can help to use a tool to identify specific issues of concern to help decide if it's time to seek professional help. Rella suggested, "If you want perspective, I would recommend that you commit to spending thirty days identifying a particular problem you're struggling with and tracking it in a journal or a spreadsheet … you could start by just writing down everything you find challenging, or habits that are causing you unhappiness, and try to distill them down into behaviors you can track. This part would be tricky, but if you are able to identify something like, 'I think about killing myself,' 'I only sleep three hours every night,' or, 'I don't leave the house because I'm worried about what people will think of me,' then those are relatively objective and observable. Then for thirty days, keep track of how often the behavior happens [and] at the end of the month, look at what you've got, and see how you feel about it. If you have [marks] for these behaviors that are causing you unhappiness more days than not, and you don't want to keep living that way, find a therapist." For more ideas on tracking your emotional state, review the section on journals.

Pagans may feel particularly guarded about sharing details about a personal religious practice with a therapist, but that will hamper the relationship. To get meaningful professional help when one is spiritually sensitive, that professional needs to understand the context. Orion Foxwood explained, "When our people walk into a therapist's office, speaking about invisible voices but not necessarily about anything that's uncomfortable, distressing, or disturbing," that counselor needs to understand if spirit contact is itself unusual rather than automatically view the situation through the Abrahamic lens that it's always problematic. "If Joe Schmo pagan tells a psychiatrist, without knowledge of our culture, that psychiatrist could severely damage our people." To make especially clear how thorny an issue this can be, Foxwood added, "There is a fine line between true spirits and hallucination, and at times as we can create spirits as humans." Having better systems for recognizing therapists familiar with these practices is crucial to the health of the community, Foxwood believes. "We don't talk about this stuff enough," and models might be found in ethnic communities where medical and spirit doctors both serve functions, such as from some Hispanic and Asian cultures. "We've got to grow language to help clinicians."

It's understandable not to want to share every intimate detail during the first session, but if religion is an important part of your life, then you need to know that your comments will be understood in context. I asked Barbara Rachel, "How can someone find a professional who doesn't harbor unconscious bias toward monotheism?"

"Finding the right therapist is a challenge for anyone, not just pagans," Rachel told me. "People, even therapists, all have biases, though therapists are supposedly trained to notice and edit theirs. It is not a matter of just one session. First of all, the client should call and speak to the person live, and have a set of questions ready. How does the therapist deal with spiritual issues? Are they comfortable listening to how a person's religion affects their emotions? It's at least a preliminary feel for the therapist's views. Then, make an appointment and talk about your views with the therapist and if it doesn't feel right, it's okay to say so and not return. If a therapist is offended with this then they are *definitely* not the one! Expect to pay for the session no matter what the outcome."

Rella advises being very clear in that first appointment. "I would recommend them being forthright in their preliminary inquiries when asking for what they want. 'I'm looking for a therapist to help me work through my depression and my ongoing conflicts with my parents. I am a pagan and it's important to me that my therapist be respectful of my religious beliefs.' Something like that." A spell to help set those expectations is in chapter nine, "Prayers, Offerings, Dreams, and Spells."

As with some energy healing techniques, therapy can be provided at a distance. Even before the pandemic led to a surge of interest, there were studies showing that talking to a therapist on the phone or a video link is as effective as being there in person, and even that asynchronous messaging therapy—using something like chat or email—can have the same benefits.[58] On the other hand, talking to friends and family via a webcam is certainly better than nothing at all, but it can be draining because it is purely a conscious activity. In person, we unconsciously process cues like body language and can use more senses to engage. Video calls are all about the eyes, ears, and attention.[59] I am incredibly grateful that we can see the faces of other people even when we don't feel safe visiting them, but it does fall short of full connection. University of Virginia psychology professor James Coan, who "studies the neural mechanisms in the brain that link social relationships to health and well-being," has found that physical contact such as holding hands or hugging alters how the brain responds to stress.[60] This particular disease attacks our social connections every bit as much as it does our lungs and hearts.

58. Novotney, Amy. "A growing wave of online therapy: the flexible nature of these services benefit clients and providers, but the onus is on psychologists to make sure they comply with federal and state laws." American Psychological Association, 48, no. 2 (February 2017): 48.

59. Sander, Libby (Elizabeth) and Oliver Bauman. "5 reasons why Zoom meetings are so exhausting." The Conversation, May 5, 2020. https://theconversation.com/5-reasons-why-zoom-meetings-are-so-exhausting-137404.

60. Entis, Laura. "The stark loneliness of digital togetherness." Vox, May 26, 2020. https://www.vox.com/the-highlight/2020/5/26/21256190/zoom-facetime-skype-coronavirus-loneliness.

✍§ JOURNAL EXERCISE §✍
Ode to a Friend

Think of someone important in your life. Set a timer for five minutes.

While the timer is running down, write as many nice things as you can about this friend or loved one. If you feel some sort of complaint rising, release it without writing about it during this time. Focus on why you enjoy this person's company, or the ways in which this person makes you a better person yourself.

Conclusion

Depression feels like a threat, and threats tend to elicit a reaction to either fight or to flee. I have done both, and neither has left me better off in the long run. While some people have but one crippling experience of this sort, for many people depression comes to visit again and again over a lifetime. Recognizing that repeating the same tactics that have failed is not wise, I have chosen to engage with depression as a spirit, and one that might not even intend to cause the harm that it most certainly does.

Our bodies, our spirits, our minds encompass a single self, and depression is a condition that impacts them all, which means that anything we do to address it on any of these levels can help ease the suffering. The unity of the self should be incontrovertible, regardless of how we conceive of its many parts and how they fit together. We use these different words to describe aspects of self, but emotions impact thinking, thinking impacts spirit, and any harm to the self eventually percolates into the body and potentially causes more harm. Whether depression intends harm or is more like an autoimmune disorder, harm results from its presence, and that harm grows over time as emotions and thoughts feed back on themselves and help create a perfect environment for this spirit by raising a dark cone of power from our own energy.

Through mindfulness we can learn to separate the voice of the spirit of depression out from the other voices that participate in the dialogue in our heads, but when it's especially tough one can lack the ability even to meditate. It is through community that we can find the support necessary to make it through those darkest hours: friends and loved ones to sit with us, gods and spirits to light the way, mental health professionals to guide and assist in our healing journey. Depression invariably leads us away from healing and instead into danger, just as toxoplasmosis will send a rat into the jaws of a hunting cat. It is through community that our runaway thoughts are slowed, our irrational impulses checked, and the negative echo chamber built by the spirit of depression is crumbled. Community includes more than just human beings, but it must include human beings to provide the most benefit.

Community is a critical support system, but in the end we must be fearless in facing this darkness. Finding a way to live with or vanquish the spirit of depression involves accepting what we do not love about ourselves and putting it into perspective. Humans are flawed, but no one reading this book is so broken that they do not deserve love and even happiness. Making peace with our mistakes and imperfections is a terrifying but necessary step on this journey. Some of those steps must be made alone, but the journey itself is one shared by all humanity. That's the secret, after all. None of us exist in a vacuum. There is always a light to guide you out of the darkness and it is always held by another. Reach for that light.

Depression Resources

Hotlines to Contact for Immediate Help

If you feel like your life is spiraling out of control and need urgent help, contact the people at any of these services. The countries are where these services originate and do not necessarily mean that only residents of that country can call.

USA and Canada

National Suicide Prevention Lifeline: 800/273-8255 (988 as of July 2022); visit suicidepreventionlifeline.org for chat in English or Spanish and for TTY information

Crisis Text Line: send the word "home" to 741741 or use the chat interface at crisistextline.org

Trans Lifeline: 877/565-8860 (US), 877/330-6366 (Canada)

Trevor Lifeline (for LGBTQ youth): 866/488-7386; chat is available at thetrevorproject.org

Veterans Crisis Line: 800/273-8255 and select option 1; send text to 838255; or chat at veteranscrisisline.net

UK

Samaritans: call 116 123 (0808 164 0123 in Welsh); visit samaritans. org for other contact options including email and postal mail

> **Tip:** If you have ever felt like you're at the end of your rope, save the number of your preferred help line in your phone with "help" as the contact name. It will be easier to get help when you need it.

Finding a Therapist for the Long Haul

A database of mental health professionals in the United States is maintained on the site for *Psychology Today*: psychologytoday.com /us/therapists.

The "Community" chapter of this book includes questions to ask a potential therapist and how to ensure a good fit.

A spell for finding a therapist can be found in the "candle magic" section of chapter nine, "Prayers, Offerings, Dreams, and Spells."

Reading Material

Facing the Darkness, by Cat Treadwell (Moon Books, 2013) weaves together experience and guidance around depression in a powerfully spiritual way.

In the Midnight Hour: Finding Power in Difficult Emotions, by Anthony Rella (Gods & Radicals Press, 2020), comes from a licensed therapist and witch.

How to Heal Yourself When No One Else Can, by Amy Scher (Llewellyn Publications, 2016) is a phenomenal book on getting oneself on the road to healing, no matter the malady.

Contributor Biographies

Anthony Rella

Anthony Rella is a witch, writer, and psychotherapist living in Seattle, Washington. He has been a full-time therapist since 2013, and his professional experience includes counseling work with men of all kinds, people in the queer community, homeless and low-income folks, chronically mentally ill individuals, and people who have been incarcerated or sentenced for criminal charges. Anthony has studied and practiced witchcraft since starting in the Reclaiming witchcraft tradition in 2005. He is a student and teacher of Morningstar Mystery School and a founding member of the Fellowship of the Phoenix's Seattle temple. His published books on psycho-spiritual healing and transformation includes *Circling the Star* (Gods & Radicals, 2018) and *In the Midnight Hour* (Gods & Radicals, 2020). More on his work is available at anthonyrella.com.

Barbara Rachel

"Though I have always been touched by the suffering of others, I was not able to be really helpful until I matured into the realization that there is really no difference between myself and people labeled as mentally ill. Thirty years ago I graduated from social work school and worked in community mental health and then found the therapy which has guided me ever since. Dialectical behavior therapy (DBT) is a skills-based treatment that is rooted in mindfulness and Buddhist thought. It has helped me and the traumatized people I work with find the path to reduce suffering and find a life worth living. I live by the four rules of life: show up, pay attention, tell the truth, and don't be attached to the results. Namaste."

Courtney Weber

Courtney Weber is a witch, author, tarot adviser, and activist. She is the author of *Brigid: History, Mystery, and Magick of the Celtic Goddess* and *Tarot for One: the Art of Reading for Yourself, The Morrigan: Celtic Goddess of Magick and Might* and *Hekate: Goddess of Witches*. She is a co-host of the "That Witch Life" podcast. She has been featured in *Maxim, Playboy, Huffington Post, Vice,* and the *Thom Hartmann Show*. Visit her online at courtneyaweber.com.

Ivo Dominguez, Jr.

Ivo Dominguez, Jr. has been active in Wicca and the pagan community since 1978 and has been teaching since 1982. Ivo is a founding member and high priest of Keepers of the Holly Chalice, the first Assembly of the Sacred Wheel coven, for which he currently serves as an elder. Ivo has been published in numerous periodicals and is the author of several books. His newest title is *The Four Elements of the Wise: Working with the Magickal Powers of Earth, Air, Water, Fire*. Find out more at ivodominguezjr.com.

Joshua Tenpenny

Joshua Tenpenny is a Freysman, a devotee of Shiva, and a retired sacred prostitute. His life is dedicated to the service of others, in various forms—through teaching and writing, as a massage therapist, as a council member of the First Kingdom Church of Asphodel, and most importantly, in his service to Raven Kaldera, helping him to change the world for the better.

Kari Tauring

Kari Tauring is a Norse cultural educator, folk musician, spiritual leader, and healer living in Minneapolis, Minnesota. She is a völva, staff-carrying woman, and the originator of the Völva Stav mind/body/spirit philosophy and practice. Growing up in a Norwegian-American ethnic enclave, Tauring began digging below the surface of her immigrant culture in 1988 when a linguistics professor introduced her to the runes. Her life's passion is to help other Americans with European roots excavate, mend, and reconnect to their own cultures of origin and the stories carried in the body through generations. Tauring maintains that reconnecting to root culture identity assists in moving us away from racialized identity. Family-of-origin stories point to the sources of trauma we carry. Root culture gives us the language, songs, dances, mythic allegories, metaphysics, and cosmologies to assist in our deep root healing. Tauring is the author of the book and iPhone app, *The Runes: A Deeper Journey*, several Nordic root musical recordings, a Nordic dance curriculum, and a series of online workshops for Nordic root healing, and maintains the website karitauring.com.

Kelden Mercury

Kelden Mercury is a traditional witch and practicing mental health therapist. He is the author of *The Crooked Path: An Introduction to Traditional Witchcraft*.

Kirk White

Kirk White, M.A., L.Ac., is a healer, teacher, author, and state legislator. He has been a registered psychotherapist since 1996 and a licensed acupuncturist/Chinese herbalist for over twenty-five years. A practicing Witch and magician since 1973, he is past co-president of Covenant of the Goddess (North America's oldest and largest association of Witches and Wiccans), and founder of both Cherry Hill Seminary, a professional pagan ministry program with faculty and students worldwide, and Standing Stone Academy, a pagan healer training program. He is author of several books on Paganism and Freemasonry.

Nimue Brown

Nimue Brown is a practicing Druid, taught by OBOD but feral in her instincts. She spends a great deal of time out of doors, reads omnivorously, is fascinated by everything, sings mournful songs, and daydreams a lot.

Orion Foxwood

Orion Foxwood is an eco-magical activist, traditional witch, conjure-man, and faery seer, and the author of *The Faery Teachings* (RJ Stewart Books), *The Tree of Enchantment, Mountain Conjure and Southern Rootwork*, and *The Flame in the Cauldron* (Weiser Books). Born with the veil in Shenandoah Valley, Virginia, he was exposed to faith-healing, root-doctoring, faery lore, and southern and Appalachian folk magic which he teaches in workshops and other forums. He is the founder of the House of Brigh Faery Seership Institute and Foxwood Temple to pass on the traditional witchcraft of his elders, and co-founder of "Conjure-Craft," "Witches in the Woods," and "The Many Roads of Faery," gatherings aimed at fostering education, community, co-creative magic, and the healing and helping practices of the traditions he carries. He holds a master's degree in human services. More can be found at orionfoxwood.com.

Raven Kaldera

Raven Kaldera is a Northern Tradition shaman, herbalist, astrologer, transgendered intersexual activist, homesteader, and founding member of the First Kingdom Church of Asphodel. He has been a practicing shaman for almost two decades now. He is the author of too many books to list here, including the *Northern-Tradition Shamanism* series, *MythAstrology*, *Pagan Astrology*, *Dealing With Deities: Practical Polytheistic Theology*, and *Hermaphrodeities: The Transgender Spirituality Workbook*. 'Tis an ill wind that blows no minds.

Sarah W.

Sarah W. is a Hellenic polytheist and devotee of Dionysos, the god who liberates minds and hearts but also heals us from destructive madness. She lives in the Pacific Northwest where she immerses herself in art, nature, and the unseen world.

Siobhan Johnson

Siobhan Johnson is a witch who focuses on the magic of stories, from archetypes to astrology and tarot, and the written word itself. She has been practicing for ten years. You can find her at siobhanjohnson.com.

Bibliography

AARP Research. The Three Generations Survey. AARP Research, September 2018. https://doi.org/10.26419/res.00249.001.

"Anti-Inflammatory Diet 101: How to Reduce Inflammation Naturally." Healthline, accessed April 18, 2021. https://www.healthline.com/nutrition/6-foods-that-cause-inflammation.

Adams, Susan. "How Unemployment And Depression Fit Together." Forbes, June 9, 2014. https://www.forbes.com/sites/susanadams/2014/06/09/how-unemployment-and-depression-fit-together/.

Anthony, Piers. A Spell for Chameleon. New York: Ballantine Books, 1977.

Association for Psychological Science. "Why Are Older People Happier?" Published January 5, 2012. https://www.psychologicalscience.org/news/releases/better-research-is-needed-to-understand-why-elders-are-happier.html.

Ballard, Byron. Staubs and Ditchwater: A Friendly and Useful Introduction to Hillfolks' Hoodoo. Asheville, North Carolina: Silver Rings Press, 2012.

Berman, Robby. "US cases of depression have tripled during the COVID-19 pandemic." Medical News Today, September 19, 2020. https://www.medicalnewstoday.com/articles/us-cases -of-depression-have-tripled-during-the-covid-19-pandemic.

Boelens, Peter A., Roy R. Reeves, William H. Replogle, and Harold G. Koenig. "A Randomized Trial of the Effect of Prayer on Depression and Anxiety." *International Journal of Psychiatry in Medicine* 39, no. 4 (2009): 377-392. https://doi.org/10.2190 /pm.39.4.c.

Bursuca, Stephanie L., and William G. Iacono. "Risk for Recurrence in Depression." *Clinical Psychology Review* 27, no. 8 (December 2007): 959-985. https://doi.org/10.1016 /j.cpr.2007.02.005.

Carhart-Harris, Robin. "We can no longer ignore the potential of psychedelic drugs to treat depression." Guardian, June 8, 2020. https://www.theguardian.com/commentisfree/2020/jun/08 /psychedelic-drugs-treat-depression.

Carr, Michelle. "What's Behind Your Recurring Dreams?" Psychology Today, November 14, 2014. https://www.psychology-today.com/us/blog/dream-factory/201411/whats -behind-your-recurring-dreams.

Choi, Karmel W., Murray B. Stein, Kristen M. Nishimi, Tian Ge, Jonathan R.I. Coleman, Chia-Yen Chen, Andrew Ratanatharathorn, et al. "An Exposure-Wide and Mendelian Randomization Approach to Identifying Modifiable Factors for the Prevention of Depression." *American Journal of Psychiatry* 177, no.10 (October 1, 2020):944-954. https://doi.org/10.1176/appi .ajp.2020.19111158.

Cunningham, Scott. *Cunningham's Encyclopedia of Crystal, Gem & Metal Magic*. Woodbury, Minnesota: Llewellyn Publications, 1988.

Dahl, Melissa. "Yes, Shopping Can Be Addictive." Elle, January 26, 2017. https://www.elle.com/fashion/shopping/a41845/shopping-dopamine/.

Davis, AK, Barrett, FS, May, DG, et al. "Effects of Psilocybin-Assisted Therapy on Major Depressive Disorder: a Randomized Clinical Trial." JAMA Psychiatry. Published online November 04, 2020. doi:10.1001/jamapsychiatry.2020.3285.

Digital Communications Division. "Does Depression Increase the Risk for Suicide?" hhs.gov. Department of Health and Human Services, August 21, 2015. https://www.hhs.gov/answers/mental-health-and-substance-abuse/does-depression-increase-risk-of-suicide/index.html.

Entis, Laura. "The stark loneliness of digital togetherness." Vox, May 26, 2020. https://www.vox.com/the-highlight/2020/5/26/21256190/zoom-facetime-skype-coronavirus-loneliness.

Fancourt, Daisy, et al. "Fixed-Effects Analyses of Time-Varying Associations between Hobbies and Depression in a Longitudinal Cohort Study: Support for Social Prescribing?" Psychotherapy and Psychosomatics (2019). DOI: 10.1159/000503571.

Ghaemi, Nassir. "Winston Churchill and his 'black dog' of greatness." The Conversation, January 23, 2015. https://theconversation.com/winston-churchill-and-his-black-dog-of-greatness-36570.

Graeber, David. *Debt: The First 5,000 Years*. Brooklyn: Melville House, 2014.

Gray, Stephen. *Cannabis and Spirituality: An Explorer's Guide to an Ancient Plant Ally*. Rochester, Vermont: Park Street Press, 2017.

Harvard Medical School website; https://hcp.hms.harvard.edu/.

Harris, Rebecca. "The Loneliness Epidemic: We're More Connected Than Ever—But Are We Feeling More Alone?" *The Independent*, March 30, 2015. https://www.independent.co.uk/life-style/health-and-families/features/loneliness-epidemic-more-connected-ever-feeling-more-alone-10143206.html.

Harrow, Judy. *Spiritual Mentoring: A Pagan Guide*. Toronto, Canada: ECW Press, 2002.

Holt-Lunstad, Julianne. "Besides Feelings Of Loneliness, What Else Does Isolation Do To Us?" Interview by Steve Inskeep. Morning Edition, NPR, June 16, 2020. Audio, 6:59. https://www.npr.org/2020/06/16/877778770/besides-feelings-of-loneliness-what-else-does-isolation-do-to-us.

Insel, Thomas R. "Assessing the Economic Costs of Serious Mental Illness." American Journal of Psychiatry 165, no 6 (June, 2008): 663-665. https://doi.org/10.1176/appi.ajp.2008.08030366.

Isaacowitz, Derek M. and Fredda Blanchard-Fields. "Linking Process and Outcome in the Study of Emotion and Aging." Perspectives on Psychological Science: January 5, 2012. https://doi.org/10.1177%2F1745691611424750.

James, Spencer L., Degu Abate, Kalkidan Hassen Abate, Solomon M. Abay, Cristiana Abbafati, Nooshin Abbasi, Hedayat Abbastabar, et al. "Global, Regional, and National Incidence, Prevalence, and Years Lived with Disability for 354 Diseases and Injuries for 195 Countries and Territories, 1990–2017:

A Systematic Analysis for the Global Burden of Disease Study 2017." The Lancet: 392:1789-1858. https://doi.org/10.1016 /S0140-6736(18)32279-7.

Kuchinskas, Susan. "Meditation Heals Body and Mind." WebMD, accessed November 12, 2020. https://www.webmd.com /balance/features/meditation-heals-body-and-mind.

Maletic, Vladimir, and Charles Raison. *The New Mind-Body Science of Depression*. New York: W.W. Norton & Company, 2017.

Merriam-Webster, s.v. "myth," accessed April 17, 2021, https:// www.merriam-webster.com/dictionary/myth.

Novotney, Amy. "A growing wave of online therapy: the flexible nature of these services benefit clients and providers, but the onus is on psychologists to make sure they comply with federal and state laws." American Psychological Association, 48, no. 2 (February 2017): 48.

Parry, Wynne. "Lice Reveal Clues to Human Evolution." Live Science, November 7, 2013. https://www.livescience.com /41028-lice-reveal-clues-to-human-evolution.html.

Pollan, Michael. *How to Change Your Mind: What the New Science of Psychedelics Teaches Us about Consciousness, Dying, Addiction, Depression, and Transcendence*. New York: Penguin Press, 2018.

Psychiatry for the People (blog). Psychiatry Today. https://www .psychologytoday.com/us/blog/psychiatry-the-people.

Raab, Diana. "What Is Centering? What Is Grounding?" Psychology Today, February 3, 2020. https://www.psychologytoday .com/us/blog/the-empowerment-diary/202002/what-is -centering-what-is-grounding.

Ratschen, Elena, Emily Shoesmith, Lion Shahab, Karine Silva, Dimitra Kale, Paul Toner, Catherine Reeve, Daniel S. Mills. "Human-Animal Relationships and Interactions During the Covid-19 Lockdown Phase in the UK: Investigating Links with Mental Health and Loneliness." Plos One: September 25, 2020. https://doi.org/10.1371/journal.pone.0239397.

Rella, Anthony. *A Site of Beautiful Resistance* (blog). https:// abeautifulresistance.org/.

Reynolds, Emily. "Phone Calls Help Create Closer Bonds Than Texting." Research Digest, October 8, 2020. https://digest.bps .org.uk/2020/10/08/phone-calls-help-create-closer-bonds -than-texting/.

Sander, Libby (Elizabeth) and Oliver Bauman. "5 reasons why Zoom meetings are so exhausting." The Conversation, May 5, 2020. https://theconversation.com/5-reasons-why-zoom -meetings-are-so-exhausting-137404.

Scher, Amy. *How to Heal Yourself When No One Else Can*. Woodbury, Minnesota: Llewellyn Publications, 2016.

Sloan, Carrie. "Why We Spend More When We're Tired (and Other Money Triggers)." The Muse, accessed April 18, 2021. https://www.themuse.com/advice/why-we-spend-more -when-were-tired-and-other-money-triggers.

Solomon, David A., Martin B. Keller, Andrew C. Leon, Timothy I. Mueller, Philip W. Lavori, M. Tracie Shea, William Coryell, et al. "Multiple Recurrences of Major Depressive Disorder." *American Journal of Psychiatry* 157, no. 2 (February 2000): 229–33. https://ajp.psychiatryonline.org/doi/full/10.1176 /appi.ajp.157.2.229.

Solomon, Andrew. " Years Ago, 'Darkness Visible' Broke Ground Detailing Depression." Interview by Renee Montagne. *Morning Edition*, NPR, December 17, 2014. Audio, 4:37. https://www .npr.org/2014/12/17/371364727/25-years-ago-darkness -visible-broke-ground-detailing-depression.

Svoboda, Elizabeth. "Gut Bacteria's Role in Anxiety and Depression: It's Not Just In Your Head." Discover, October 4, 2020. https://www.discovermagazine.com/mind/gut-bacterias-role -in-anxiety-and-depression-its-not-just-in-your-head.

Szabo, Allyson. *Longing for Wisdom: the Message of the Maxims*. United States: Bibliotheca Alexandrina, 2008.

Tannenbaum, Melanie. "'But I didn't Mean It!' Why It's So Hard to Prioritize Impacts Over Intents." *Scientific American*, October 14, 2013, https://blogs.scientificamerican.com/psysociety/ e2809cbut-i-didne28099t-mean-ite2809d-why-ite28099s-so -hard-to-prioritize-impacts-over-intents/.

Treadwell, Cat. *Facing the Darkness*. UK: Moon Books, 2013.

Truschel, Jessica. "Depression Definition and DSM-5 Diagnostic Criteria." Psycom, accessed November 12, 2020. https://www .psycom.net/depression-definition-dsm-5-diagnostic-criteria/.

U.S. Department of Health & Human Services. "Does Depression Increase the Risk for Suicide?" Mental Health & Substance Abuse. Content last reviewed September 16, 2014. https:// www.hhs.gov/answers/mental-health-and-substance-abuse /does-depression-increase-risk-of-suicide/index.html.

Vale, V. and John Sulak. *Modern Pagans: An Investigation of Contemporary Practices*. RE/Search Publications: San Francisco, 2001

Vedantam, Shankar, host. *Hidden Brain: A Conversation about Life's Unseen Patterns.* "Did That Really Happen? How Our Memories Betray Us." Aired December 16, 2019 on NPR. https://www.npr.org/2019/12/16/788422090/did-that-really-happen-how-our-memories-betray-us.

Wanck, Bick. *Mind Easing.* Deerfield Beach, Florida: Health Communications, Inc., 2019.

Ward, Terence P. (as Terentios Poseidonides). *Depth of Praise: A Poseidon Devotional.* CreateSpace, 2016.

White, Kirk. *Advanced Circle Magick: Essential Spells and Rituals for Every Season.* New York: Citadel Press, 2007.

To Write to the Author

If you wish to contact the author or would like more information about this book, please write to the author in care of Llewellyn Worldwide Ltd. and we will forward your request. Both the author and the publisher appreciate hearing from you and learning of your enjoyment of this book and how it has helped you. Llewellyn Worldwide Ltd. cannot guarantee that every letter written to the author can be answered, but all will be forwarded. Please write to:

Terence P Ward
℅ Llewellyn Worldwide
2143 Wooddale Drive
Woodbury, MN 55125-2989

Please enclose a self-addressed stamped envelope for reply,
or $1.00 to cover costs. If outside the U.S.A., enclose
an international postal reply coupon.

Many of Llewellyn's authors have websites with additional
information and resources. For more information,
please visit our website at http://www.llewellyn.com.